TEXAS
OFF-ROAD RACING 2

THE BATTLE FOR ATV AND SIDE-BY-SIDE CHAMPIONSHIPS

MIKE KOWIS, Esq.

TEXAS OFF-ROAD RACING 2:
The Battle for ATV and Side-by-Side Championships

Copyright © 2023 Mike Kowis, Esq.

All rights reserved. No part of this book may be reproduced or transmitted in any form or by any means, electronic or mechanical, including photocopying, recording, or by any information storage and retrieval system, without the written permission of the publisher except where permitted by law.

Library of Congress Control Number: 2023913505
ISBN-13: 978-1-7328630-7-1 (paperback)
ISBN-13: 978-1-7328630-6-4 (eBook)

www.mikekowis.com

Lecture PRO Publishing
Conroe, Texas

Dedication

This book is dedicated to Terry Deck and Cory Williams for creating an exciting new ATV and side-by-side series in Texas so off-road racing fanatics like my son and I have a place to play in the dirt.

May God bless you and the TX4 Cross-Country Series!

Testimonials

Here's what people are saying about *Texas Off-road Racing 2*:

"What does Mike know about racing? He thought beadlocks was a hairstyle." – Mike's barber

"This book does for off-road racing what Crocs did for the fashion industry." – a disappointed racing fan

"Speaking of paper weights, *Texas Off-road Racing* 2 is perfect." –Mike's supportive mom

"We had to wait 36 long years for the *Top Gun* sequel, but only 3 years for *Texas Off-road Racing 2*." – President of Mike's fan club

"Ugh… not another book!" – Mike's literary agent

"Growing up, Mike had a promising writing career. So much for that!" – Mike's 8th grade English teacher

"A sequel to *Texas Off-road Racing*? Are we not giving him enough work to do at the office?" – Mike's day job boss

"Off-road racer? The only thing 'off' about Mike is his sense of humor." – the Baja 1000 Grand Marshal

"Another *Texas Off-road Racing* book? Does he need more papers to grade?" – College President where Mike teaches

But seriously, you're gonna love this thrilling book. Go ahead and read it now… I double-dog dare you!

Contents

INTRODUCTION 1

CHAPTER 1: Diamond Willow 7

CHAPTER 2: Powell Ranch 21

CHAPTER 3: Sand Dune Trip 33

CHAPTER 4: Knesek Ranch 43

CHAPTER 5: Powell Ranch 2.0 53

CHAPTER 6: Diamond Willow 2.0 67

CHAPTER 7: Let's Ride Ranch 83

CONCLUSION 91

BONUS CHAPTER: Cash's First ATV Race! 95

LET'S GET CONNECTED 105

ACKNOWLEDGEMENTS 107

ABOUT THE AUTHOR 109

INTRODUCTION

2022 started with a gut punch as the off-road racing series that I belonged to for the previous five years announced they would no longer host side-by-side ("SxS") races. This decision was soul-crushing for many die-hard racing enthusiasts like myself because it apparently meant no more SxS cross-country ("XC") racing in Texas. Regardless, I'll always be grateful to the Texas Off Road Championship Series ("TORCS") for giving Texas SxS racers the opportunity to play in the dirt from 2017 through 2021. Together with my son (Cash) as my lucky co-pilot, we won the TORCS Turbo SxS Championship in 2019 - the subject of *Texas Off-road Racing: A Father-Son Journey to a Side-by-Side Championship* – and again in 2021. More important, we met tons of great people who treated us like family and made countless father-son memories that will last a lifetime.

Luckily, the Texas XC racing community is a resilient bunch who aren't afraid to get busy when things get tough. Terry Deck and Cory Williams quickly filled the void by organizing a new off-road racing series in the Spring of 2022. With Cory's help, Terry created the TX4 Cross-Country Series ("TX4") to host thrilling races in central Texas for both SxSs and all-terrain vehicles ("ATVs"). For more info, check out www.TX4racing.com.

Cory Williams (left) and Terry Deck (right), promoters of the TX4 Cross-Country Series. Photo courtesy of Davey Kroll with DK28 Photography.

These two unassuming heroes were the perfect duo to take on this challenge because both worked tirelessly behind the scenes to design and build awesome SxS tracks for the TORCS series. They also helped their fellow racers in any way they could. In fact, both gentlemen helped Cash and me limp our broken side-by-side back to the trailer a time or two.

When the new TX4 series was first announced in January 2022, the possibility of racing both a SxS and an ATV was all I could think about for the next few weeks. At that point, I had not thrown my leg over a quad since 2014 when I crashed my 2007 Kawasaki KFX 700 into a barbed wire fence during a Texas Off-Road Nationals ("TORN") race held in north Texas. As explained in *Texas Off-road Racing*, that traumatizing wreck resulted in a broken right wrist, a bruised ego, and marked the end of my ATV racing career forever… or did it?

In the immortal words of famous radio host, Paul Harvey, "And now for the rest of the story." Finally, I got the nerve to ask my beautiful bride of 24 years what she thought about me racing quads again. She said, "yes, just don't wreck!" With Jessica's stamp of approval, I started the hunt for the perfect utility quad for me to race. After consulting with friends and the "all-knowing" internet, I found the perfect 4-wheel drive quad – a 2021 Canam Renegade 1000r Xxc - at a local ATV dealership. It was previously-owned with only 11 original miles on the odometer and still looked brand spanking new. A few days later, it was parked in my garage. The purchase was the easy part. Now I had less than three months to prep it for XC racing and get some seat time before the first TX4 race scheduled for late April.

What follows is the wild ride that Cash and I shared racing our SxS together during the 2022 TX4 season and camping under the stars at the race tracks - complete with howling coyotes and crowing roosters in the background. It also chronicles my attempt at quad racing after an eight-year hiatus in not just one, but two ATV classes. But wait, there's more! You don't want to miss the Bonus Chapter because it covers Cash's first ever ATV race during Round 1 of the 2023 TX4 season. Now let's get this party started.

TX4 competitors proudly standing for the National Anthem before the start of an ATV race / Photo courtesy of Mike Kowis.

TX4 WHEEL CROSS COUNTRY SERIES
APRIL 23-24, 2022 — ROUND 1
DIAMOND WILLOW
738 FM 969 BASTROP TX 78602

WEEKEND SCHEDULE:

FRIDAY - GATES 2:30 - 11 pm
REGISTRATION 4 - 8 pm

SATURDAY - GATES 7 - 11 pm
REGISTRATION 7 - 6 pm

SUNDAY - GATES 7 - 2 pm
REGISTRATION 7 - 12 pm

ATV RACING

- **8 - 8:30** MINI PRACTICE
- **9am** MINI RACE (30 min)
- **10 - 10:30** AMATEUR PRACTICE
- **10:30 - 11** EXPERT / PRO PRACTICE
- **11:30** VINTAGE / OPEN C / UTILITY 40+ AM / BLASTER / ATC / WOMEN (60 min)
- **1 pm** PRO (90 min) OPEN A / OPEN B / 40+ EXPERT / UTILITY EXPERT (70 min)
- **3:00** PT QUAD LINEUP / SIGHT LAP
- **3:15** PT QUAD RACE (30 min)
- **4:15** ATV PODIUM (30 min)
- **5:00** POKER RUN / TRACK CRAWL ($20 per hand)

UTV RACING

- **8:30** MINI UTV SIGHT LAP
- **9:00** MINI UTV RACE (30 min)
- **10:00** SIGHT LAP FOR ALL ADULT UTVs
- **10:30** WOMEN / 50+ / 800 / SPORTSMAN BEGINNER RACE (60 min)
- **12:30** PRO / TURBO OPEN / NA OPEN
- **1:40** OPEN CHECKERED FLAG
- **2:00** PRO CHECKERED FLAG
- **2:30** ALL UTV PODIUM

RACE FEES

- **GATE FEE** $10 — UNDER 8 / OVER 60 FREE
- **CAMPING** $20
- **MEMBERSHIP** $40
- **FULL SIZE ATV** $50
- **PRO ATV** $75
- **MINI ATV** $30
- **FULL SIZE SXS** $90
- **PRO SXS** $180
- **MINI SXS** $40

SPIDER WILLIAMS 1943-2021 MEMORIAL RACE
"YOU CAN'T WIN THE RACE ON THE FIRST LAP... BUT YOU SURE CAN LOSE IT."

CHAPTER 1:
Diamond Willow

The sweet smell of race gas filled the air on the morning of April 23, 2022. That's the day TX4 kicked off its inaugural season of XC racing in the Lone Star State. The internet buzz leading up to this event paid off in spades as the ATV community showed up in full force that Saturday with 55 entries, including mini quads. The impressive turnout should not have been a surprise given that XC racing for quads had been extinct in Texas for the prior six years. During this dry spell, dedicated ATV racers travelled all the way to Oklahoma, Arkansas, and Louisiana to get their cross-country racing fix. Many others switched to SxS or dirt bike racing, or simply stayed home.

Equally excited for this weekend were the 25 SxS competitors (including minis) who thought their days of XC racing were dead and gone just a few months earlier. Their season officially started the following day - Sunday, April 24th.

When the alarm clock sounded Saturday morning at 6:10 a.m., I was already wide awake and pumped to go racing again. Within 30 minutes, I was on the road with "Big Blue" (my trusty 2018 Polaris RZR Turbo) and the "Couch Rocket" (my now race-prepped 2021 Canam Renegade) loaded on a 20-foot open trailer. Two and a half hours later, I arrived at the Spider Williams Memorial Race (Round 1 of the 2022 TX4 series) held at Diamond Willow in Bastrop, Texas.

TRACK CONDITIONS

Having raced on this property several times during the last five years with the TORCS series, Cash and I have grown accustomed to seeing it under one extreme condition or another. It's usually either dry and dusty or wet and muddy. This year, Mother Nature gave us a bone-dry track with tons of blinding dust. These conditions typically mean less than ideal viewing opportunities for spectators and potentially dangerous conditions for competitors. But it wasn't all bad news as the temperatures were mild and a constant breeze lifted the dust away in the open pasture areas. However, thick clouds of dust seemed to hang endlessly in wooded sections, making it extra challenging for racers with limited visibility to dodge trees.

According to the Couch Rocket's odometer, the ATV track was 5.7 miles long and included plenty of tight, twisty trails through the woods, sweeping turns through open, bumpy pastures, plus a half dozen or more dry creek crossings. The SxS course was laid out along most of the ATV track (minus a few sections of tight woods) for a total of 5.1 miles. Compared to the previous SxS races hosted here by the former series, this course was longer, included more tight woods, and was marked better. Overall, the course was fast, fun, and not too technical for newbie racers.

ATV CLASSES:

For Round 1, TX4 offered an ATV class for everyone including young kids, old geezers like myself, pros, women, vintage quads, 3-wheelers, utility quads, and Justin Bieber fans. Okay, maybe the last class is not real, but I heard my long-time ATV racing buddy, Matt Horton, was trying to organize that class because he's got BIEBER FEVER, baby!

TX4 also offered a nice variety of SxS classes too, including mini SxSs for the little ones, seniors (I said, "SENIORS" for those old folks who can't hear me), women, beginners, 800cc SxS, non-aspirated SxS, Turbo SxS, and a Pro SxS class.

Of course, all classes were subject to change depending on turnout. If racers wanted these classes, they had to show up on race day and do their part to spread the word about this awesome new XC series.

ATV PRACTICE:

Before the 10 a.m. ATV practice session began, each quad was required to go through technical inspection. During inspection, a TX4 staffer and fellow quad racer, Zach Racette, carefully looked over the quad's brakes, steering, kill switch, and other major components to make sure it was in good working order and capable of safely competing on the course. Once each quad passed inspection, Zach placed a colored zip tie on the handle bar and wished the racer good luck.

For this inaugural event, minor hiccups were anticipated. And it didn't take long for the first minor problem to occur. ATV practice started a few minutes late and the first slow lap (called a "parade lap") was a bit confusing at times. The leader accidentally led the parade lap off the marked track a few times and then turned the entire group around to correct course. After the somewhat chaotic parade lap, ATV racers continued practice at their own pace and everything went smoothly thereafter.

During practice, racers could feel the adrenaline rush as dozens of ATVs and 3-wheelers (also referred to as trikes, all-terrain cycles, or "ATCs" for short) revved their 2-stroke and 4-stroke engines and zig-zagged their way around the twisty track. For a while, I followed an old trike as it bounced along the trail (keep in mind that ATC suspension is primitive and relies heavily on their balloon tires) and it brought back wonderful memories of my teenage youth. Back then, I spent countless hours exploring the wooded trails along the Trinity River on my first three-wheeler – a red 1984 Honda 200s. Fun times!

A half-mile into the parade lap, I was suddenly reminded that I was riding an ATV (not a side-by-side) when my helmet tagged a low hanging tree branch as I passed underneath. It quickly got my attention, and I laughed out loud upon realizing that I forgot to duck.

A few hundred yards up the trail, I sped around a bumpy corner a bit too fast and my Renegade jostled me side-to-side like a rag doll in a pit bull's mouth. I somehow managed to hang on and bring it back down on all four wheels, but not before Terry (who was resetting track markers nearby) saw me and started laughing. I pulled over, and he jokingly reminded me that I don't have a roll-cage on my ATV. Point well taken!

After practice, things started to set in that I'm finally racing an ATV again after an 8-year hiatus. As mentioned above, the last time I raced a quad was the summer of 2014 when I rolled my Kawasaki KFX700 through a 4-strand barbed wire fence during a TORN race held at Red River Motorcycle Park. My wife was not thrilled that I came home with a broken right wrist and she said, "no more ATV racing" for me. Hence the reason I started SxS racing in 2015 and continued doing so in both the TORN and TORCS series. To be frank, I never thought I'd see the day when I'd be racing an ATV again. And I certainly didn't foresee a time when I'd compete in both ATV and SxS races during the same weekend. What a blessing!

TRACK DESCRIPTION:

The starting line was located in a small, grassy field near the scoring chute. From there, racers headed straight for 100 feet before making a hard right turn around a tall tree ("Turn Number 1"). Next, the course zig-zagged around a few more big trees in the open area before making a sweeping left-hand turn and ducking into the first wooded section.

Soon afterwards, the track popped into the open field again near Turn Number 1, made another zig-zag turn around tall trees and then headed back into the tight, twisty woods again. After dodging several trees, racers entered a small open section before slamming on their brakes, maneuvering through a small, dry ditch and immediately turning left into the next set of woods.

Another ten yards up the trail, it made a 90-degree right turn and immediately dropped down into a dry, 10-foot deep ditch and climbs up the other side.

Next, racers entered a large grassy field where they zig-zagged between mature oak trees randomly scattered here and there. Eventually, the track ran back into another section of tight woods and came out near a small pond on the far side of the same large, grassy field. From there, the track zig-zagged through the bumpy field towards the front of the property, ran in and out of woods adjacent to the parking lot area, and ended up at the scoring chute.

ATV RACE:

Not long after ATV practice ended, Cash arrived at the track to watch my ATV race and take pics. He drove in from the college that he was attending at that time, which was located just 50 minutes away.

We watched the start of the 11:30 a.m. race, which included the Trikes, Vintage class, Blaster class, Open C, Utility Amateurs, 40+ Amateurs, and the Women class. Cash was surprised to see a few racers get off their vintage quad or 3-wheeler to physically push them backwards towards the starting line when they accidentally pulled forward a bit too far. I explained that most older quads and 3-wheelers didn't have a reverse gear. Or as Terry later explained, "Yeah, we were men. We pushed everything!"

When it was time for the 1 p.m. ATV race to begin (which actually started around 1:50 p.m.), they lined up the Pro class on the front row followed by Open B, 40+ Expert, and finally the Utility Expert class in the back row. Sadly, I was the only competitor in Utility Expert on this day. Racing alone in my class took some of the fun out of it. But on the bright side, it also took the pressure off to get on the podium and allowed me to focus on running a clean race. One other racer signed up for this class, but he left before the race began due to a sudden medical issue. At that point, I was a little disappointed with the lack of competition in my class and started regretting that I didn't sign up for the Utility Amateur class, which had a solid turnout at the 11:30 a.m. race. Regardless, I was just glad to be racing on a quad again!

Just little ol' me racing the Couch Rocket at the Diamond Willow ATV race. Photo courtesy of Davey Kroll with DK28 Photography.

Overall, my first round ATV race went smoothly with little fanfare. Except for getting lapped by the Pro racers, I didn't see much racing action. On the plus side, that meant I didn't have to eat much dust. In fact, the biggest challenge I had was keeping my new riding pants from falling down. About half way through the race, I felt a cool breeze on my backside and realized I was unwittingly mooning nearby spectators. Talk about embarrassing!

From that point on, I sat down whenever I drove past a spectator unless I was holding my pants with my left hand. Lesson learned… I'll wear suspenders next time.

Despite my best efforts to keep up the pace, my lap times deteriorated as the 70-minute race wore on. My lack of conditioning really showed towards the end. By the fifth lap, my arms and legs were burning, painful blisters had formed on both hands from the death grip I had on the handlebars, and I was praying to see the checkered flag as soon as possible. Turns out that was my final lap, and I was so relieved to be done!

SATURDAY NIGHT:

Around 7 p.m., Cory led a dozen side-by-sides plus a few dirt bikes for the first TX4 poker run. This slow, leisurely event was a great way to unwind after an intense and exhausting day of ATV racing. It also gave SxS racers a sneak peak of their course to be run the next day. I wasn't sure if I'd enjoy it or not, but decided to give it a try as I had nothing better to do, and Cash had already left for the day.

Once we got moving along the SxS course, Cory would occasionally stop the winding train of off-road vehicles and ask each participant to pick a lucky card from the deck. At the end of the course, whoever drew the best poker hand won half of the total entry fees collected for that event, and the rest of the money supported the TX4 series. Despite ending up with a losing hand, I thoroughly enjoyed this relaxing event and the opportunity of getting to know my fellow racers better. In fact, I liked it so much that I decided to enter all future TX4 poker runs.

Because I will race both days and gasoline wasn't currently cheap, I decided to camp overnight at the track on Saturday evening. This was my first ever attempt at primitive camping, and I felt nervous about my lack of proper equipment and limited preparations. In fact, I was far more anxious about camping than racing. I invited Cash to join me, but he wisely chose to drive back to his apartment where he could enjoy a hot shower and a comfy bed. Maybe he's learning something at that college after all.

Rather than buy an expensive tent and all the trappings that come with it, I chose a simple 10-foot by 10-foot canopy and set it up directly above my 20-foot open trailer so that I didn't have to sleep on the ground with all of the creepy, crawly things. Next, I set up a hammock directly under the canopy. Other than an occasional weekend cat nap in the backyard, I've never tried to sleep in a hammock. Turns out, it's probably not a bad choice if you can sleep on your back. However, I prefer to sleep on my side and I gave up after an hour of unsuccessfully trying to fall sleep.

Plan B was to ditch the hammock for an old air mattress that I brought from home. So, I grabbed a flashlight and stumbled my way to the truck. Once I retrieved the air mattress, I slowly aired it up with a foot-operated air pump. I soon realized this manual pump was taking way too long, so I switched to lung power. Twenty minutes of huffing and puffing later, I finally got it filled. Ahhh… finally time to catch some Zs. Or so I thought.

Alas, my troubles were not over. A short time later, I felt the hard trailer floor through the sagging air mattress and realized it had a slow leak. For the rest of the evening, I climbed out of bed every few hours to top off the air mattress and then tried to get some shut eye. It was a miserable experience, but motivated me to prepare better for Round 2.

I present to you the "Luxury Suite" at Hotel Kowis. Electricity, running water, and air conditioning not included / Photo courtesy of Mike Kowis.

SxS PRACTICE:

On Sunday morning, the SxSs had a single parade lap at 10 a.m. Just like Saturday's ATV practice, you could feel the energy from all of the racers. It was great to be back on a SxS course with many of my racing buddies from the former series.

Unlike Saturday's ATV parade lap, this one went off without a hitch. The course looked nearly identical to the ATV race except for missing some of the tight wooded section that previously ran along the edge of the parking lot. There were no hot laps allowed, so I immediately went back to my truck afterwards to top off the fuel, clean the air filter, check tire pressure, and wait for Cash to arrive at the track.

SxS RACE:

When 12:30 p.m. rolled around, Cory turned on the microphone and gathered the SxS racers for a short rider's meeting near the starting line. After explaining the general rules and reminding everyone to turn on their chase lights, he gave a final piece of advice that stuck with me for the next 70 minutes. His words of wisdom went something like, "If you finish the race, you'll probably make it on the podium." In other words, avoid the trees, don't do anything stupid, and you'll probably see the checkered flag. Turns out, that was excellent advice.

Because there were only three competitors in my Turbo SxS class, it meant we would all end up on the podium if we avoided a DNF status, meaning "did not finish." The "if" was critical.

Then, Cory lined up four Pro SxS competitors on the front row, three Turbo SxS racers on the second row, and separated the 11 racers in the naturally-aspirated ("NA") SxS class into three separate rows.

The Pro SxS class did a live engine start, and the rest of the SxS classes started with a dead engine. The live engine start for the Pro class was exciting to watch, but it was a bit unusual given that most XC races (including the Grand National Cross-Country Series or "GNCC" for short) use a dead engine start.

After the Pros took off, Cash and I pulled Big Blue to the right side of the starting line. To my immediate left was Lane McGinnis and to his left was Phil Waggoner. Cash and I said a quick prayer for the safety of all racers and finished with our lucky fist bump. Now we were ready to rock!

The flag went up and off we went. Big Blue started slow like usual, but somehow we got off the line first, which almost never happens. Woo hoo!

Cash and I were both excited to win the holeshot (meaning the first racer to make it around Turn Number 1) and then we enjoyed clean air for the next few turns. Soon, we entered the first section of woods with two hungry Turbo SxSs snapping at our rear bumper. I knew there was no room to pass anyone in these woods, so I decided to keep a steady pace and buy some time until I could get to the open sections and try to put some distance on Lane and Phil.

About a mile or so into Lap 1, the trail shot out of the woods and made short jog through an open section and then ran through a dry ditch. On the other side of the ditch, the trail made a hard right into a small section of woods and then ran through another dry ditch before entering an open field. As we passed through this wooded section and approached the second ditch, I suddenly heard a loud CRUNCH coming from the direction of the right rear fender of Big Blue. I asked Cash about the mysterious sound and he didn't know either. I was concerned that I might have clipped a tree or broke something. All I could do was keep going and hope for the best. Luckily, Big Blue felt normal, and I kept the hammer down.

On Lap 2, I discovered the alarming noise came from Lane getting a bit too friendly with a tree. That collision ended his race early, and he got the dreaded DNF. In fact, his car was still stuck on the trail and wedged between two small trees. Luckily, there was just enough room on the left side to squeeze by and proceed on the course. Seeing this, I was instantly reminded of Cory's sage advice - finish the race and you'll probably get on the podium.

Cash and I racing Big Blue at Diamond Willow / Photo courtesy of Thomi Beadnell.

As Cash and I approached the scoring chute at the end of Lap 2, Cory yelled that a car from another class was right behind us. So, I quickly pulled into the pit area to let the NA racer pass. Then I jumped behind him and started Lap 3 at my regular pace. I would have gladly pulled over sooner, but couldn't tell what class he was in due to the heavy dust.

A minute later, I noticed a car approaching in my rearview mirror and thought it was another NA car. So, I purposely drove wide around the next turn to let him easily pass. As soon as I did, I realized my mistake. I just handed the lead to our remaining competitor, Phil. Doh!

I felt like an idiot. Only 30 seconds later, Phil checked out and was gone! Feeling a bit defeated, I thought this turn of events was probably for the best because Phil was clearly running faster through the tight trees than I was comfortable going. In any case, my goal had not changed. Stay the course and finish the dang race… just like Master Cory advised.

On Lap 4, I passed the same tree where were I accidentally let Phil take the lead one lap earlier and noticed a car stopped ahead near the edge of the woods. As we got closer, I realized it was Phil's car. Oh, my goodness! After we passed him, Cash and I fist bumped to celebrate our good fortune of retaking the lead. Not knowing what kind of damage Phil had, I was still concerned he might get his car repaired soon and catch up. One lap later, we noticed Phil's car still in the same spot, which basically meant we had already won the race. Yee-haw! Sometimes, it's better to be lucky than good.

According to the official results, I took first place in the Utility Expert ATV class and both Cash and I took the win in the Turbo SxS class. Congrats to Phil for finishing second place in the Turbo SxS class, and I wish Lane better luck at the next one (but not too much luck!). Most important, my son and I had a blast that weekend, and I didn't break any bones. At that point, we were already looking forward to Round 2.

Starting with the left side, Cory Williams is interviewing second place finisher Phil Waggoner (sponsored by Woods Cycle Country). On the right side, Cash and I are taking home first place in the Turbo SxS class at Diamond Willow / Photo courtesy of Davey Kroll with DK28 Photography.

TX4 CROSS COUNTRY SERIES
MAY 21-22, 2022 — ROUND 2
POWELL RANCH
573 HIGH GROVE RD. CEDAR CREEK, TX 78612

WEEKEND SCHEDULE:

FRIDAY - GATES 2:30 - 11 pm
REGISTRATION 4 - 8 pm

SATURDAY - GATES 7 - 11 pm
REGISTRATION 7 - 6 pm

ATV RACING
- **8 - 8:30** MINI PRACTICE
- **9am** MINI RACE (30 min)
- **10:15 - 11** ADULT ATV PRACTICE
- **11:30** VINTAGE / OPEN C / UTILITY 40+ AM / BLASTER / ATC / WOMEN (60 min)
- **1 pm** PRO (90 min) OPEN A / OPEN B / 40+ EXPERT / UTILITY EXPERT (70 min)
- **3:00** PIT QUAD LINEUP / SIGHT LAP
- **3:15** PIT QUAD RACE (30 min)
- **4:15** ATV PODIUM (30 min)
- **5:00** POKER RUN / TRACK CRAWL ($20 per hand cash only)

SUNDAY - GATES 7 - 2 pm
REGISTRATION 7 - 12 pm

UTV RACING
- **8:30** MINI UTV SIGHT LAP
- **9:00** MINI UTV RACE (30 min)
- **10:00** SIGHT LAP FOR ALL ADULT UTVs
- **10:30** WOMEN / 50+ / 800 / SPORTSMAN BEGINNER RACE (60 min)
- **12:30** PRO / TURBO OPEN / NA OPEN
- **1:40** OPEN CHECKERED FLAG
- **2:00** PRO CHECKERED FLAG
- **2:30** ALL UTV PODIUM

RACE FEES
- **GATE FEE** $10 (UNDER 6 / OVER 60 FREE)
- **CAMPING** $20
- **MEMBERSHIP** $40
- **FULL SIZE ATV** $50
- **PRO ATV** $75
- **MINI ATV** $30
- **FULL SIZE SXS** $90
- **PRO SXS** $180
- **MINI SXS** $40

CHAPTER 2:
Powell Ranch

On Saturday, May 21st, Cash and I left home at the crack of dawn with Big Blue and the Couch Rocket in tow. We eagerly drove to Powell Ranch in Cedar Creek, Texas for Round 2 of the 2022 TX4 cross-country series. My lucky co-pilot and I had been looking forward to another fun weekend of off-road racing and primitive camping since last month's inaugural event. Compared to Round 1, this event had a similar turnout with 49 ATVs and 25 SxSs competing, including minis.

TRACK CONDITIONS

Mother Nature must've been off her meds this weekend because the weather couldn't have been more different. Saturday felt like the middle of summer with high humidity and temps reaching 99 degrees. The intense heat plus bone dry soil conditions equal tons of thick dust for racers to contend with. Later that night, a thunderstorm dumped a few inches of wet stuff and Sunday's competitors enjoyed cool temps (mid-70s) and "hero dirt" (perfect soil conditions with no mud or dust).

The ATV and SxS courses were very similar and each consisted of 3.6 miles of twisty wooded trails, zig-zag runs between tall trees in the open areas, and a handful of creek crossings. The track layout flowed well included plenty of tight trees and natural obstacles to keep racers on their toes.

ATV PRACTICE:

On Saturday morning, ATV racers met up with Zach for a quick tech inspection and then headed to the starting line for practice at 10:15 a.m.

As I slowly zig-zagged my way around the ATV track for the first time, one thing that struck me was the huge variety of machines on the course. Some rode modern machines (like the Couch Rocket), which had power steering, drive-by-wire technology, water-cooled twin cylinders, EFI, etc. Others piloted vintage quads from the 1980s with old school technology – think air-cooled, single-cylinder engines with a carb and kick-starter. Most rode quads, but a handful of brave souls maneuvered the course on just three wheels. Many machines were powered by 4-stroke engines, while others had 2-smokes… err, I mean 2-stroke engines. Together, we were a motley crew with one common interest – our love of Justin Bieber! Err… I mean our passion for XC racing.

The other thing I noticed during the ATV practice lap was how much fun it was to navigate my quad through the tight woods, open fields, and multiple creek-crossings. In addition, the course had plenty of obstacles including cactus, low-hanging tree limbs, stumps, ruts, barbed wire fences, and other hazards. This track was not scary or super technical, but it definitely required racers' full attention at all times.

ATV RACE:

Because I was the only person registered for the Utility Expert class again, they let me register in the Utility Amateur class to race with a few other competitors. This change meant I'd be racing in the late morning rather than the afternoon. This sounded great to me because it was already 90 plus degrees when the 11:30 a.m. race began, and the temps would continue to climb for the afternoon race.

Joining me in the Utility Amateur class were two racers sharing the same first name. Sean Cowart rode a Canam Outlander 1000r, which is similar to my quad.

On the other hand, Sean Burnett showed up with an old school utility quad. Most folks know the Honda Rancher 350 is a capable machine, very reliable, and has been around forever. In fact, I read somewhere that Davy Crocket once rode a Rancher into the battle of the Alamo (which might explain why it ended so badly). In any case, the Rancher is not sporty in any sense of the word and has about as much suspension as my Craftsman riding lawnmower. Needless to say, it takes big balls to ride this mini-tank in an hour-long XC race.

Our class lined up on the fourth row behind the Open C, Vintage, and the 40+ Amateur class. Behind us were the Blasters, Trikes, and the Women class. When it came time for the Utility class start, Sean B. was lined up on the far left, Sean C. took the middle spot, and I grabbed the far right position. The first right-hand turn was approximately 60 feet ahead of us.

Once the green flag came up, Sean B. immediately shot off the line. I jumped out a half-second later and quickly passed him. I took the holeshot, and both Seans followed me around Turn Number 1.

Here I am racing the Couch Rocket in the Utility Amateur ATV class at Powell Ranch. Photo courtesy of Davey Kroll with DK28 Photography.

After Turn Number 1, I followed the wide track as it wound back and forth through a bumpy field lined on the edges with tall grass and patches of thick underbrush. Soon, the course took racers into the woods where it immediately dropped down into "Cory's Gulch" – a short drop off on one side and then a fairly steep hill climb up the other side. The tricky part was squeezing between a few trees on the way up and immediately making a hard right around a tree at the very top.

Next, racers were treated to more twisty trails through the tight woods and bumpy fields. About halfway through the course, the track pops into a field with large trees scattered here and there. Racers zig-zagged between these large trees while dodging low-hanging limbs. On the second lap, I didn't notice one of these limbs (which resembled a fork with broken tines) until the last second. I tried to duck, but got slapped on the side of my helmet. I was uninjured, but it woke me up and forced me to pay more attention to the course for the rest of the race.

Because I held the lead position, I enjoyed clean air for most of my race except for times when I caught up to a lapper (a slower racer). Eventually, I ran across a young lady sitting on a blue Raptor 90 near the bottom of a dry creek crossing. I wasn't sure if she needed help, so I pulled over to ask if she was okay. She shook her head to indicate, "no." Then I asked if she needed a medic and she shook her head to indicate, "yes!" I told her I'd get help for her soon and took off. When I reached the scoring chute a half-mile up the trail, I relayed the info to the track officials and then proceeded with my race. I later heard that someone else found her and helped get her quad back on the track so she could proceed with her race.

On Lap 5, I started feeling uncomfortably hot and a bit dizzy. To beat the sweltering heat, I planned to sip water from my camelback at least once every lap whether I was thirsty or not. It was during my fifth lap that I realized I had forgotten to drink during the last few laps and the heat was getting to me. I immediately consumed water and removed my goggles to get more airflow into my helmet. Not feeling 100 percent, I also decided to slow my pace a bit. A half-lap later, I started feeling normal again and picked up the pace.

On the sixth and final lap, my old bones were feeling dog tired. I found myself making slight mistakes and getting sloppy around turns. I nearly tagged a tree or two and realized I needed to refocus until the end of the race. I was so relieved when I finally saw the checkered flag at the end of that lap!

SATURDAY NIGHT:

Around 6 p.m., Terry slowly led a dozen side-by-sides around the SxS track for another fun poker run. Cash drove Big Blue while I sipped on a cold adult beverage from the co-pilot's seat. We ended up with two losing poker hands, but had lots of laughs along the way. Cash was caught off guard by one of the dry creek crossings on the track, but he handled it smoothly. As we slowly climbed through another creek crossing, we suddenly saw a stray cow hanging out by a small pool of water next to the dry creek. Luckily, Mr. Cow was not around come race time the next day, or else we might have had hamburgers for Sunday dinner.

Based on my lousy Round 1 experience, my camping game is clearly not as strong as my racing skills. This time, Cash and I both slept under our 10' x 10' canopy set up above our open trailer. But this time I upgraded bedding with the purchase of two roll-out matrices made of thick material similar to memory foam. While not cheap, this set-up easily beat the two options I tried to sleep on last time.

However, my sleeping woes were not yet over. The biggest problem we encountered this time was the weather. After reaching a whopping 99 degrees on Saturday afternoon, the temps were still a balmy 80 plus degrees around 10 p.m. Even with small battery-powered fans, it felt like a sauna lying there under the canopy. All we could do was wait for the rainstorm predicted to hit sometime that night.

Soon, Cash and I saw lightning strikes in the distance, but we weren't close enough to hear thunder. Mother Nature teased us for an hour and then downpours finally began around 11:30 p.m. It rained hard, the wind blew strong, and thunder boomed all around us. Surprisingly, Cash and I stayed relatively dry for the first ten minutes. Eventually, the howling rain made its way under the vent flaps on top of our canopy and started dripping down on us. Ugh. Then I remembered the plastic tarps I bought in case things got bad, but they were still inside the cab of my truck. Unfortunately, it was too late to retrieve them without getting soaked to the bone. So, we stayed hunkered down and rode out the storm.

Twenty minutes later, I received a text from our camping neighbor and fellow SxS racer, Bubba Belaire. He asked if we were staying dry under our canopy. I said no, but assured him that we'd survive. Bubba replied that his tent was taking on water, but he and his brave wife, Susan, would probably float away on their air mattress if things got any deeper. LOL

About an hour later, the storm calmed down to a light rain and temps quickly dropped 10 degrees or more. The rain finally stopped around 2 a.m., leaving Cash and me shivering under our wet bed sheets. So, I retrieved two dry bed sheets plus an emergency blanket from my truck. I gave Cash one sheet and the blanket. I kept the other dry sheet for myself and finally drifted off to sleep. We woke up around 8 a.m. to the gentle sounds of mini-UTVs firing up in preparation for their morning race. Woo hoo! We survived the night.

SxS PRACTICE:

On Sunday at 11 a.m., the SxSs had a parade lap plus one optional hot lap. A few tight spots (like Cory's Gulch) were cut out, but otherwise the SxS track looked identical to the ATV course. In the middle of the parade lap, Cash and I followed the line of cars through an open gate and then zig-zagged through a rectangular field. Near the far side of the field, Cash and I observed a large turtle briskly crawling away from the track. Hmm. Could that be a sign we were going to be S-L-O-W as a turtle in this race, or did it mean we'd come from behind like The Tortoise and the Hare? Read on to find out!

Terry Deck (right) chatting with Davey Kroll (left) before the SxS Practice at Round 2. Photo courtesy of Scott Hardy.

After completing the parade lap and hot lap, we went back to the truck to prepare Big Blue with more fuel and check tire pressure. After killing a little time, we suited up and headed to the starting line.

SxS RACE:

When 12:30 p.m. rolled around, Cory called out to the SxS racers for a short rider's meeting near the starting line. While listening to Cory, two more competitors joined us on the Turbo SxS line. That made a total of five cars in our class. Hooray! That's an improvement over the last race, which only had three racers.

Then Cory lined up four Pro SxS competitors on the front row, five Turbo SxS racers on the second row, and separated the 12 racers in the naturally aspirated class into three separate rows.

Like last time, the Pro SxS class elected to have a live engine start. Bubba grabbed the holeshot and the early lead. The rest of the SxS classes started with a dead engine, just as God and nature intended!

After the Pros took off, Cash and I pulled Big Blue to the starting line. We were in the middle of the line and angled a bit to the right. Unfortunately, there was not enough room between the cars on my left and right to reverse and square up on the line. So, I stayed put and hoped for the best.

Lane and Phil, both of whom competed in Round 1, were lined up to my left side. To my right were a few newbies, including David Holybee and Chris Donald. Cash and I said a quick prayer for the safety of all racers and finished with our lucky fist bump. Now it was GO TIME, baby!

The flag went up and off we went. David's Can-am X3 on my immediate right quickly pulled off the line before I could get Big Blue going and he accidentally bumped my front right tire as he went by. Luckily, it didn't do any damage, and we were able to continue racing… which was a big relief!

David won the holeshot followed closely by Lane. As I approached Turn Number 1, I saw Phil coming up fast on my left. I had the inside line, so I held it and made it around the first turn in third position. Phil was immediately behind me and Chris took the last position.

For the first mile or so, our class hung together in a tight pack. With everyone clinging to the bumper of the next guy, it made passing nearly impossible.

In the middle of Lap 1, racers ran though tight woods and made a sharp left-turn between two small trees. On the backside of this turn was a six-inch tall stump that was easy to hit if you weren't careful.

After that turn, the course went straight for 25 yards and made another 90-degree left turn. To get around this tight corner without backing up, you had to swing wide to the right and then duck between the two small trees on the left as you exited the turn. This turn was extra tricky for me because I had raced between the two trees on the right during Saturday's ATV race. That line was too narrow for SxSs, hence the need to go left around this turn. For every lap, I had to remind myself that this turn was different for the SxS race.

Immediately past this turn, the trail widened and went straight over whoops for 20 yards and then narrowed down to only 1-car width as it ran between small trees. Just before Cash and I reached the end of that whoops section, Phil quickly passed on our right. I was shocked because I never saw him coming. And I was impressed because he timed the pass perfectly before reaching the narrow path through the small trees. Regardless, I had to slam hard on my brakes to avoid hitting his left rear tire. That pass left Cash and me in fourth position. Yikes!

Our class continued to run bumper-to-bumper for the next mile. At that point, Phil appeared anxious to pass and grab second position from Lane. But there was not much room to do so in the woods. Finally, the trail ducked out of the trees and made a hard right turn into an open grassy section. Next, the trail made a hard left around a wooden stake and generally headed towards another section of woods. Just ahead, there was a long white ribbon strung between a wooden stake and a small tree that directed racers to the left of the tree. Just past that tree, the course headed to the right where it re-entered the woods. Phil took that opportunity to pass Lane on the right side of the ribbon. I wasn't sure if that move was legal, but I later saw a Pro racer do the same thing, so it was probably fair game. In any case, I played it safe and followed Lane around the small tree.

Immediately after Phil's pass, David held the lead, followed closely by Phil, Lane, me, and, finally, Chris. Soon thereafter, our class started to spread out as Phil put some distance on Lane and me.

Cash and I piloting Big Blue in the Turbo SxS class at Powell Ranch. Photo courtesy of Davey Kroll with DK28 Photography.

SxS LAPS 2-7:

Cash and I continued to follow Lane and kept him within eye-sight for a few laps. I felt confident that I could probably catch and pass Lane when it was safe to do so. However, the longer the race continued, the more my suspension started to fade. By Lap 3, it felt like I blew a rear tire or the rear sway bar broke. Big Blue was getting harder to control and bounced all over the track at times. Then I started to lose confidence and backed off the pace a bit. The last thing I wanted to do was push the car too much and wreck it.

In the middle of either Lap 3 or Lap 4, Cash and I entered the rectangular field where we saw the turtle during practice. At that point, we were following closely behind a young driver (Riley C.) in the naturally-aspirated class who had just passed us. Riley's Polaris RS1 went a bit too wide around a sandy turn and fish-tailed a bit. Just as he did, a huge cloud of fine sand erupted into the air and enveloped his RS1. He literally disappeared from view for a half-second like some kind of David Copperfield magic trick. It was surreal!

When the official results were posted on Saturday, I took the win in the Utility Amateur ATV class, Sean C. placed second, and Sean B. finished in third place. My hat goes off to both guys for running a solid race in brutal heat.

On Sunday, Cash and I finished a disappointing fourth place out of five competitors in the Turbo SxS class. Congrats to Phil, David, and Lane for taking first, second, and third, respectively. Cash and I inspected Big Blue after the race and found nothing broken but our pride. The fading suspension was a sign that it was time to refresh the shocks. In fact, it had been three years since George White at Double E Racing re-valved and re-sprung them, so it was way passed time to do that. I planned to get that done this coming summer and then try for better results at Round 3.

Even though Cash and I didn't finish on the podium, I'm happy to report that we accomplished our two goals for the weekend. The first goal was to have fun (check!) and the second was to avoid any damage to our off-road vehicles so we could take them to the Little Sahara Sand Dunes the following month to celebrate Cash's 21st birthday (double check!).

CHAPTER 3:
Sand Dune Trip

On Friday, June 10th, Cash and I hit the road to Little Sahara State Park in Waynoka, Oklahoma. Ten hours later, we reached the 1,600-acre off-road park in northern Oklahoma, which is quite popular for side-by-sides, quads, and sand rails. Cash's 21st birthday was the perfect excuse for us to visit this place for the first time ever.

Cash and I are happy to reach the entrance of Little Sahara State Park.
Photo courtesy of Mike Kowis.

DAY 1:

After driving all day, we finally arrived at our rental cabin in Waynoka just before nightfall. We were full of excitement and there was no way we were going to wait until morning to check out the park. So, we immediately unloaded Big Blue for a night ride.

Lucky for us, we were able to legally drive our off-road vehicles from our cabin to the park's entrance via a designated dirt trail that was established for this purpose. By the time we reached the entrance, bought tickets, and entered the park, the sun was already gone. After meandering around in the dark for the first 30 minutes, we finally found a fun spot where we could ride up and down the steep side of a 50-foot sand dune. Flying down the steep side of that dune felt just like a roller coaster, and we rode it a half-dozen times while screaming like little kids. It was a blast!

Then it was Cash's turn to take the wheel. Once strapped in to the driver's seat, he steered us up the side of the same hill from the opposite direction. I could tell that his approaching speed was too slow. Just as we began climbing the side of the hill, Cash let off the gas pedal and Big Blue immediately started tipping over towards my side of the car. The next few moments seemed to happen in super slow motion as our RZR laid over onto its passenger side. At that moment, I vividly remember thinking to myself that we needed to keep our hands and arms inside the cab at all times because our window nets were not up to protect us. Luckily, the impact was not jarring as Big Blue topped over onto soft sand.

The moment we came to a complete stop, Cash and I were suspended by our 4-point seat harnesses. I quickly unbuckled mine and crawled out of the front opening of the cab where a windshield would normally be on an automobile. Then I noticed the engine was still idling, so I reached inside the cab and turned off the ignition key. Next, Cash unbuckled his harness and climbed out. I remember being surprised at how calm both of us were despite this being the first time either one of us were involved in a SxS roll-over.

With Big Blue's headlights, light bar, and rear chase lights still on, Cash and I walked around the vehicle to inspect its post-crash condition. All kinds of possible damages were running through in my mind (e.g., broken ball joints, bent tie rods, flat tire, etc.), and I was beginning to wonder if our dune trip was over before it really began. After a quick inspection, we decided it was both good news and bad news. On the plus side, we found no major damage that would prevent us from continuing our night right. The bad news was that Big Blue was sitting completely on its right side with the front end tilted slightly downhill. In this position, there was no way the two of us could physically lift our 1,500-pound vehicle back onto four wheels. We tried once, and it didn't budge an inch.

At that point, we desperately needed to find help. Our toppled SxS left us stranded in the dark with no idea where the park entrance was located even if we wanted to walk back to the cabin. In the distance, I could see the headlights of a few side-by-sides playing in the dunes. So, I grabbed the flashlight from Cash's camelback and started waiving it towards their general direction.

Within a few minutes, a friendly guy named Colton and his buddy showed up in a pair of SxSs and offered to upright our rig. Colton drove his RZR Turbo around the backside and up to the top of the tall dune immediately above us. Then Cash crawled up the steep, soft slope to retrieve the winch cable coming from Colton's front bumper. A few minutes later, Colton winched Big Blue onto four wheels again, and we were back in business.

Upon further inspection, we discovered the only damage was cosmetic - a small dent to the right side of the metal roof. What a relief! I offered Colton some money for helping us out of a jam, and he adamantly refused. Cash and I felt grateful that this little incident turned out to be nothing more than a learning lesson for Cash (keep your speed up when ascending hills at an angle) and it didn't end our adventure prematurely.

Cash ready to take Big Blue on a night ride in the sand dunes. Photo courtesy of Mike Kowis.

Afterwards, we thanked our new friends and then proceeded to explore the park alone with just the moonlight (which was now peeking out from the clouds) and Big Blue's lights to guide our path.

The further we drove into the park, the less vehicles we saw. In fact, we started feeling alone and desolate at times, as if we had the entire park to ourselves. As we continued exploring the open dunes and the wooded trails along the edge of the park, we'd occasionally see a small group of riders in the distance. But they often disappeared into the darkness just as quickly as they first appeared. Sometimes the clouds blocked the moonlight and it became impossible to see much beyond the reach of our headlights. This was both scary and exciting because we didn't yet know our way around the park, much less how steep the next downhill descent was. So, we pressed on into the night with a cautious speed.

Eventually, we found ourselves on the other side of the park and realized we were totally lost. We tried to get back to the side where we entered the park, but had no idea how to get there. The rolling dunes looked the same after a while, and the wooded trails along the edges of the park looked sketchy in places. I ventured into the wooded trails a bit, but didn't go far. I couldn't risk getting stuck in the soft sand or flipping over again, so we turned around at the first sight of anything ahead that looked technical or sketchy. We continued to search for a way back to the park entrance. This continued for 90 minutes, and I started feeling frustrated and hopeless.

At one point, we found an entrance, but soon realized it was not the same one we used to enter the park. We tried using Google maps on our cell phones, but it was completely useless because it had no details about the inside of the park or where the two entrances were located. To be fair, this problem was partly my fault because I forgot to drop a pin on the map when we entered the park. Doh!

Eventually, we caught up to a group of SxSs and ATVs and asked for directions. They seemed friendly, but started arguing on the best way to reach the other entrance. At that point, I felt even more hopeless and was sure we'd have to wait for the sunrise before we'd be able to find our way back to the cabin. Finally, they agreed to let us follow them around the park until they reached our entrance. However, they warned us to keep up with them, and they took off in a hurry. They were regular visitors and drove up and down the steep dunes at blazing speeds. As newbies, Cash and I were apprehensive about climbing and descending the dunes in the dark, especially at fast speeds. They were scary enough at slow speeds.

Soon, the group started to leave us in the dust. They quickly ascended a steep dune in front of us and their taillights disappeared as they dropped over the crest. As much as I wanted to find another way around, I knew that we had no choice but to follow in their tracks up and over that dune. So, we held our breath as we climbed to the top and then took the plunge down the other side of that tall sand dune. And we did so at fast pace so as not to get left behind. Talk about scary!

Sometime around midnight, the group we were following finally reached the entrance that we were desperately hoping to find. Like before, we offered money for their trouble, but they refused again and again. It was impressive to find such friendly riders who are truly in it for the fun and comradery.

DAY 2:

The next morning, Cash and I hopped on our ATVs (my Couch Rocket and Cash's 2008 Honda trx250ex) and headed back to Little Sahara State Park. Riding in the daytime was a totally different experience because we could clearly see our surroundings and the actual height of each dune. We climbed to the top of the taller dunes – some over 75 feet high – just to take in the views of the rest of the park. During this visit, we were extra careful to keep track of the park entrance at all times so as not to get lost again. At lunchtime, the thermometer reached a toasty 95 degrees, so we decided to head back to the cabin for sandwiches and cold air conditioning.

Temps reached a blazing 102 degrees that afternoon, so we stayed indoors and played cards or read books to pass the time. After dinner, it finally cooled off to more palatable 90 degrees. With an hour of sunlight left, we headed back to the park in Big Blue.

As we approached the park entrance, we noticed dark smoke clouds ascending from somewhere inside the park. I asked a park ranger about it at the entrance gate, but he said it was probably something outside the park and nothing to worry about.

As we entered the park, we headed towards the smoke. A few minutes later, we rode up on a crazy scene that I'll never forget. A dozen people were standing around a campfire… only that was no campfire! Rather, it was a smoldering 2021 Polaris RZR Turbo S. The tires and other flammable components were already disintegrated, and we watched as the rest of the machine quickly burned down to just the charred remains of the frame and metal wheels. The metal roof had melted under the intense heat and folded inward like a soft candle. I found the distraught owner standing next to the flaming wreckage and asked him about it. He explained that the fire started while a friend was driving it slowly, and they had no idea what caused the fire to ignite. Sadly, the one-year-old RZR only had 5 hours of use and - even worse - he didn't have insurance on the vehicle. Talk about an expensive day at the dunes. Yikes!

Soon, it was dark and we continued exploring the park with our lights on. Unlike the night before, I paid careful attention to where we were in relation to the park entrance, and we didn't get lost this time.

DAY 3:

After a quick 9 a.m. breakfast, we rode Big Blue into the park for more fun. At that point, we were finally feeling comfortable carving up the dunes and climbing/descending steep slopes. At noon, outdoor temps reached triple digits and we headed back to our cabin to cool off. Later that afternoon, it reached a blistering 108 degrees, so I'm glad we took a break when we did.

That night it cooled down to a "chilly" 83 degrees, and we took our quads on a night ride for the first time. To find our way in the complete darkness of the dunes, Cash and I wore halogen lights attached to our helmets. Helmet lights are necessary in the dunes because the stock ATV headlights don't typically spray a wide-angle light and are not helpful if the rider wants to look for a path off to one side or the other. We found that our helmet lights worked well at slow speeds, but you could outdrive them at a faster pace. Both lights were supposed to shine for a minimum of 3 hours, but one of them ran out of "Edison juice" after 90 minutes. At that point, we were getting tired anyway and decided to head home while we still had one good helmet light to guide our path.

DAY 4:

Just like before, we spent our final day riding the dunes in the morning and again at night to avoid the 105-degree temps in the afternoon. By this time, we finally memorized our way around the 1,600-acre park in the daylight and moonlight too.

In addition to the intense heat, we also had to deal with 30 to 40 mph winds on the last day. On the plus side, the gusty winds leveled out the surface until it felt smooth as glass. This made the ride even better, especially at high speeds. On the other hand, there's nothing fun about getting sand blasted in the face while riding 70 mph across the flat dunes. Unfortunately, our off-road helmets and goggles didn't prevent the airborne sand from stinging the sides of our faces and any exposed skin. The crazy winds also stirred up the sand at times and made it challenging to see. In fact, it sometimes looked like we were driving through a thick fog.

Cash and I taking in the views of the surrounding dunes / Photo courtesy of Mike Kowis.

In total, Cash and I rode 250 miles in Little Sahara State Park. Every mile was great fun, except for the time Cash accidentally laid Big Blue on its side. Regardless, this dune trip was the perfect way to celebrate Cash's 21st birthday, and I hope we come back someday.

DAY 5:

After loading up the truck and trailer early in the morning, we began our 10-hour journey home. The long drive was uneventful except for running out of fuel two miles before reaching the Oklahoma-Texas border. There wasn't a gas station within sight, but I remained calm because I knew we had a few gallons left in the spare gas cans that we carried for the ATVs and Big Blue. It only took a few minutes to add this fuel to the truck's tank, and we were on our way again.

CHAPTER 4:
Knesek Ranch

After the long, hot summer break, TX4 racers were chomping at the bit for more racing action. Luckily, Round 3 races held on September 24th and 25th at Knesek Ranch in Rockdale, Texas didn't disappoint. ATV attendance numbers were close to the last round with 47 quads (including minis) competing. However, the SxS numbers were down to only 13 competitors due to conflicts with other SxS races held that weekend.

Cash and I previously raced on this property several times with the former series and always enjoyed it. Our last visit to this property in March 2021 was memorable because we lost the left rear wheel during the race, which ended our day early. Afterwards, Terry was kind enough to help us limp Big Blue back to the trailer on just three wheels. To do that, Cash drove slowly while I stood on the passenger side nerf bars (outside of the vehicle) to get the weight off the left, rear of the car where the wheel was missing. With that disappointment in mind, my only two goals for Round 3 were having fun and finishing each race with all four wheels attached. I'm happy to report that Cash and I checked both boxes.

Yours truly kicking up dust at Round 3.
Photo courtesy of Davey Kroll with DK28 Photography.

TRACK CONDITIONS

Saturday and Sunday were warm (mid-90s) with sunny skies. The hot, dry weather meant racers must deal with dust on the track again. Luckily, a constant breeze carried it away quickly in most areas.

The ATV and SxS courses were similar except for a different section of woods near the first mile or so. The quad track was 3.8 miles long and the SxS track was 3.4 miles. Both tracks started with several zig-zag turns in the open pasture area, and then ran though tight, twisty woods on the far right side of the property. Finally, the last two miles ran through a sparse wooded section on the left side of the property before returning to the starting line area. Overall, the track was fast and flowed well. The bumpy pasture trails were wide and had plenty of sweeping turns. The woods were littered with tire hazards, such as prickly cacti, thorny mesquite trees, small stumps, and tree roots. Those obstacles and the occasional low-hanging branch kept racers hyper-focused on the trail ahead at all times. Just one slip up could result in a DNF at best, or a costly repair or medical injury at worst.

ATV PRACTICE:

On Saturday morning, ATV racers met up with Zach again for tech inspection and then headed to the starting line for 10:15 a.m. practice.

As I slowly snaked around the ATV track on the Couch Rocket during the parade lap, I immediately noticed the first mile was much different than the previous races held there. Never before had we ventured into the woods on the right side of the pasture, so this section was new and exciting. On the other hand, the rest of the course felt familiar in terms of the terrain and track layout.

Another thing I noticed was how tight the new wooded section was. On the first practice lap, I had to stop and back up because I didn't turn sharp enough to get through an "S" curve lined on each side with thick underbrush and small trees. Obviously, stopping and backing up is no bueno during a race. So the solution was to quickly crank the handle bar from side to side in order to pass that section without getting hung up.

During the first practice lap, I let John Glover (a fellow Utility Amateur ATV class racer) pass me in the woods. Unbeknownst to me, he hit a tree soon thereafter and rolled his Polaris Sportsman 850. Luckily, both he and the quad were unscathed. Unfortunately for him, that was a sign of things to come.

ATV RACE:

Joining me in the Utility Amateur class on this day were three other brave souls. As usual, Sean Burnett showed up to race on yet again another vintage utility quad. This time, he brought a 16-year-old Bombardier 400. It's hard to believe, but this dinosaur of an ATV was an improvement over the last race when he rode an old Honda Rancher 350. Joining him for this event was his brother Gene Burnett on a Kymco 500 plus Sean's good buddy, John Glover. The four of us were a motley crew, and we were eager to tear up the course.

The Utility Amateur Class lined up on the last row behind the Open C, Vintage, 40+ Amateur, Blasters, and Trikes. When it came time for our class to start, I lined up the Couch Rocket on the far right side while facing the first left-hand turn approximately 75 feet ahead.

As Cory pointed to each rider on the starting line, I nodded my head to indicate I was ready and then focused my attention on the green flag he was holding. As soon as he waved it in the air, I hit the start button and shot off the line. John had a good start too and we both took the early lead towards the first turn. I barely grabbed the holeshot followed closely by John. Sean and Gene followed suit. Woo hoo! So far, so good.

John Glover in hot pursuit of me and the Couch Rocket in Round 3.
Photo courtesy of Davey Kroll with DK28 Photography.

After Turn Number 1, the track repeatedly zig-zagged through the large grassy field towards the front of the property. A half-mile later, the course took racers into the tight woods where the super tight "S" curve was located. I carefully maneuvered through it without incident and continued onwards. Yeehaw!

While flying through the woods as fast as I dared go, I heard one of my competitors coming up on my rear bumper. I was too focused on the course ahead to look back, so I wasn't sure who it was. Suddenly, I heard a loud hissing sound and instantly thought I popped a rear tire. There was no time to pull over and check, so I kept pushing forward and waited to see how the Couch Rocket handled.

A few turns later, the course dumped riders back into the large open field, and I was relieved to discover my quad felt normal and undamaged. More important, the rider who was previously on my tail had vanished as quickly as he appeared. After the race, I found out it was John who caught me in the first section of woods. While attempting to pass me, John got cozy with a fence post and flipped his utility quad. When he finally got the machine upright again, he discovered a damaged valve stem for one of his tires. This explains the loud hissing sound I heard. With John out of the race, that left Sean and Gene in hot pursuit behind me. However, I had no idea John was done for the day and kept the hammer down in case he was still chasing me.

As I entered the scoring chute at the end of Lap 1, I tried to grab the small water hose connected to my camelback so I could sip some water. To my surprise, I couldn't reach it and signaled Chad Williams, a TX4 staffer and fellow SxS racer, for help. He handed it to me on the right side and as soon as I let go, it immediately moved back out of reach again. Ugh. At that point, I was highly concerned about finishing the race without access to my water supply.

At the end of Lap 2, I stopped next to Chad again, and he quickly untangled the hose and moved it to my left side. It was a huge relief to regain access to my water supply.

The second half of the race was mostly uneventful except for passing a few of the slower racers from other classes. Some pulled off the trail quickly and let me pass, while others made me work for it. I always smile whenever I approach a trike during practice because it reminds me of the fun times I had riding my three-wheeler in the mid-1980s. However, it was beyond frustrating to eat a trike's dust for two miles during a race until I could finally find a safe place to pass in the woods. Grrr.

As the race wore on, I grew tired and looked forward to finally seeing the checkered flag. When I pulled into the scoring chute at the end of Lap 5, I was hoping to see Chad waiving that flag. Instead, he was waiving a finger in the air as if to signal "one more lap." Ugh! I had a finger that I wanted to show him. LOL

After completing all six laps, I ended up with the win, Gene finished second place, and Sean took third place. Congrats to both of them.

SATURDAY NIGHT:

At 7 p.m., Terry slowly led a dozen side-by-sides and ATVs around the SxS track for another relaxing poker run. To my surprise, this little event became one of my favorite parts of the TX4 race weekend. As mentioned above, the poker run is a great way to unwind after a hard day of ATV racing and also a good excuse to socialize with fellow racers and their families. Just as important, SxS competitors get a sneak peak of their track, which usually varies slightly from the ATV track.

On this evening, the pot of entry fees reached a whopping $400. Half of it goes to one lucky winner and the other half supports the TX4 series. Congrats to John Glover for having the best poker hand and taking home the cash prize on this evening. Gene Burnett also won a free T-shirt for getting the next best hand. Win or lose, everyone enjoyed lots of friendly conversation and a few cold beverages.

Afterwards, I returned to my trailer where I enjoyed another night of primitive camping next to the track. While it wasn't quite as hot as Round 2, this evening was still warm with nearly 80-degree temps at midnight and only a few battery-powered fans to keep me cool. Things got interesting just after midnight when a nearby train rolled through. Its loud horn was startling, but not as disturbing as what I heard next. Several coyotes somewhere in the dark woods behind me began howling, and I was instantly reminded that I wasn't alone. Camping in the open without so much as a flimsy tent to separate me from the wild animals, I felt vulnerable and climbed inside the safety of my truck. Five minutes later, I came to my senses and realized I couldn't fall asleep in the front seat of my truck. So, I reluctantly went back to my bed on the open trailer and tried to put on a brave face.

Around 3 a.m., another train rolled through, and my heart started pumping hard again at the sound of more coyotes howling nearby. I stayed in my bed this time and tried to get some shut-eye. Despite feeling exhausted and sleepy when the sun came up, I was never so happy to get out of bed.

SxS PRACTICE:

On Sunday morning around 10 a.m., the SxSs had a parade lap plus one optional hot lap. As expected, the track looked similar to the ATV course with the exception of a new section of tight woods near the first mile of the track. To enter this wooded section from the field, racers ran through an opening in the fence line. The fence post on the left side of the opening was loosely wrapped with barbed wire and stuck out in places. If racers got too close, it would easily shred their tires.

After completing the parade and hot lap, I went back to the truck and topped off Big Blue's fuel and tire pressure. After killing a little time, I suited up and headed to the starting line. Let's do this!

SxS RACE:

When it came time to start the SxS races, Cory lined up the sole Pro competitor (Terry) on the front row, then two Turbo racers (John and me) on the second row, and divided the half-dozen racers in the Naturally Aspirated class into two separate rows.

After Terry took off, I pulled Big Blue to the right side of the starting line and John and his co-pilot lined up their 2021 Turbo RZR on my left. I said a quick prayer for the safety of all racers, and then it was time to put on my game face.

The flag went up and off we went. John got off the line slightly ahead of me and quickly moved in my direction to get a good angle around Turn Number 1. With him blocking my direct path to the first turn, I had no choice but to let off the gas pedal and fall in line behind him.

John Glover and his co-pilot taking the early lead over me in Round 3. Photo courtesy of Davey Kroll with DK28 Photography.

After John took the holeshot, I followed him through the grassy field and a half-mile later we entered the first wooded section. At that point, I was only a few car lengths behind him. Soon thereafter, I could tell he was quickly pulling away from me. By the time I entered the second set of woods, I was only seeing John's dust in the air. Gulp! But I didn't panic. I just reminded myself that XC is an endurance race, not a sprint. Anything can happen in 70 minutes, and I wasn't about to throw in the towel yet.

Halfway through Lap 1, I spotted John through the trees and counted 16 seconds until I reached that point. After I exited the scoring chute and started Lap 2, I spotted John again in the open field as he was headed into the woods. I counted 35 seconds until I reached that point and realized there was no way

I could catch him if he kept up that pace. My only hope was that he might have a mechanical issue or tag a tree. Sadly, I never saw John again until I finally reached the finish line following 10 laps of hard racing.

I later found out that John got a flat tire in the middle of the race and pulled over to change it. His lovely bride, Jodi Roush, and a handful of close friends changed the tire so fast that NASCAR called them afterwards to ask for tips. Despite his unplanned pit stop, John still managed to easily beat me by three and a half minutes. My hat goes off to John for taking the convincing win.

TX4 CROSS COUNTRY SERIES
OCTOBER 29 - 30, 2022 — ROUND 4
POWELL RANCH 2.0
573 HIGH GROVE RD. CEDAR CREEK, TX 78612

WEEKEND SCHEDULE:

FRIDAY - GATES 2:30 - 11 pm
REGISTRATION 4 - 8 pm

SATURDAY - GATES 7 - 11 pm
REGISTRATION 7 - 6 pm

ATV RACING
- **8 - 8:30** MINI PRACTICE
- **9am** MINI RACE (30 min)
- **10:15 - 11** ADULT ATV PRACTICE
- **11:30** VINTAGE / OPEN C / UTILITY 40+ AM / BLASTER / ATC / WOMEN (60 min)
- **1 pm** PRO (90 min) OPEN A / OPEN B / 40+ EXPERT / UTILITY EXPERT (70 min)
- **3:00** PIT QUAD LINEUP / SIGHT LAP
- **3:15** PIT QUAD RACE (30 min)
- **4:15** ATV PODIUM (30 min)
- **5:00** POKER RUN / TRACK CRAWL ($20 per hand cash only)

SUNDAY - GATES 7 - 2 pm
REGISTRATION 7 - 12 pm

UTV RACING
- **8:30** MINI UTV SIGHT LAP
- **9:00** MINI UTV RACE (30 min)
- **10:00** SIGHT LAP FOR ALL ADULT UTVs
- **10:30** WOMEN / 50+ / 800 / SPORTSMAN BEGINNER RACE (60 min)
- **12:30** PRO / TURBO OPEN / NA OPEN
- **1:40** OPEN CHECKERED FLAG
- **2:00** PRO CHECKERED FLAG
- **2:30** ALL UTV PODIUM

RACE FEES
- **GATE FEE** $10 (UNDER 10 / OVER 60 FREE)
- **CAMPING** $20
- **MEMBERSHIP** $40
- **FULL SIZE ATV** $50
- **PRO ATV** $75
- **MINI ATV** $30
- **FULL SIZE SXS** $90
- **PRO SXS** $180
- **MINI SXS** $40

CHAPTER 5:
Powell Ranch 2.0

October 29th and 30th was an amazing weekend of off-road racing at Round 4 of the 2022 TX4 cross-country series. This exciting event was held at Powell Ranch for the second time that season, and the weather could not have been more perfect. In addition to California weather, racers enjoyed "hero" dirt, which I'm pretty sure stands for "Heroic Effort Racing Opportunity."

Despite having raced at this property just five months earlier, the ATV and SxS courses felt completely different because they were run in the opposite direction and more than a mile of new trails were added. This event had 39 ATVs and 19 SxSs (including minis) competing, which was similar to the total number of racers in Round 3.

TRACK CONDITIONS:

The weather gods were smiling down on TX4 because rain fell on this property just a few days prior to this event and daily temps ranged from mid-70s in the daytime to low-50s at night. The result was superb racing conditions, meaning traction was ideal and there was very little mud, dust, or heat exhaustion to worry about. Speaking of perfect weather, I have often noticed that old dogs are more energetic and playful when cooler weather arrives, and the same is true for old racers like myself. In fact, I felt so good after my Saturday morning ATV race that I raced again in the afternoon (more on that later). Yippee!

As usual, the ATV and SxS courses were fairly similar except for a few wooded sections. The ATV course had 4.7 miles of twisty wooded trails, zig-zag runs through open areas, and a handful of dry creek crossings. The track flowed well except for the super tight stuff that caused racers to slow down or else risk tire or tie rod damage. The tight woods, small jumps, cacti, random holes, deep sandy ruts, stumps, and other natural hazards kept racers on their toes at all times. The SxS course included 4.3 miles of the same types of obstacles, but had its own tight wooded section.

Here I am racing in the Utility Expert ATV class at Powell Ranch 2.0. Photo courtesy of Jodi Roush.

ATV PRACTICE:

On Saturday morning, ATV racers checked in with Zach for tech inspection and then headed to the starting line for practice at 10:15 a.m.

As I slowly zig-zagged my way around the ATV track for my first practice lap, one thing that struck me was how much longer and how different this course felt compared to the last time we raced here in May. I also noticed a few small areas with standing water and sloppy mud, so that meant tear-offs would be a good idea (at least for the first few laps until the racers splashed the water out of the holes). The last thing I noticed was how tight the new wooded sections were. In one place just past the zig-zag turns in a small, square pasture, the trail made a 90-degree right turn at the end of a short straight section surrounded by several small trees. The utility quad in front of me couldn't get around this turn without backing up once, and I had the same bad luck. Uh oh… backing up during a testosterone-fueled race is not ideal, so I would have to figure out that corner and soon.

MORNING ATV RACE:

In the 11:30 a.m. race, the Utility Amateur class had five competitors, including John on his Canam Renegade 1000r Xmr, Sean B. on a Polaris Scrambler 850, Gene on a Kymco 500, a new guy named Chris Cluck on a CFMoto 400, and myself on the Couch Rocket.

Our Utility Amateur class lined up behind the 40+ Amateur, Open C, and Trikes and the Vintage quads started behind us. When it came time for my class's start, I was lined up in the middle with two quads on my left and two on my right. The first right-hand turn was approximately 60 feet ahead of us.

When Cory waved the green flag, I quickly shot off the line and grabbed the holeshot. Woo hoo! Even with a strong start, Sean and John were hot on my heels and I knew I'd have to keep the pace up if I was going to hold the lead.

After Turn Number 1, the track wound back and forth through a bumpy, open field adjacent to the parking lot. One-quarter-mile up the trail, it made a hard left turn around a small tree and then dropped into a small, shallow area filled with sloppy mud. After a few zig-zag turns around large trees, the course made another left and crossed a deep, dry creek crossing. I still held the lead at that point, but knew that Sean and John were close behind me just itching for a chance to pass.

Soon, I caught up to some of the slower racers in the Trike class. Catching this class was inevitable as most of them are racing on 40-year-old machines with small motors and little-to-no suspension. The first trike didn't seem to notice I was on his rear bumper and no amount of yelling or revving my motor seemed to get his attention. At that point, I had most of the Utility Amateur class on my rear bumper, and we were all eager to get around this guy. Finally, I found a wide enough area to make a safe pass on his left and then headed towards the next right-hand turn around a small tree. Just as I reached the outside turn around that tree, John passed me on the inside of that tree. That was a smart move on his part, and I wish I had taken that line.

Now in second position, I reminded myself that it's a long race and there's no reason to panic. A few hundred yards up the trail, we entered an open section that runs back and forth between large pecan trees. At that point, I was caught behind another slow trike and again he didn't seem to mind the entire utility class on his rear bumper. I finally found a wide enough spot to safely pass him and moved to my right to set up for the pass. Suddenly, Sean moved to the left and quickly passed the trike on that side. Sean's pass threw off my timing for a split second, and then I tried to make my move. Suddenly, I noticed a small tree ahead that blocked my path, so I had to fall behind the slow trike once again. Ugh!

After the next left-hand turn, I was finally able to get around him. However, Sean had already grabbed a big lead over me and was already in the next section of woods. Grrr.

After five laps of hard racing, I finished in third place. Congrats to John for taking the win and Sean for finishing a close second place. Both were running 12-minute lap times on average, which was 90 seconds faster than my average pace. My hat goes off to both of them.

AFTERNOON ATV RACE:

Because the weather was so nice and I still felt good after the first race, I decided to sign up for the Utility Expert class starting at 1 p.m. I've always wanted to do the "Matt Horton special" (racing both ATV races on Saturday like my old friend Matt always does), but never had the energy to try it before. Now was the perfect time to give it a go!

Also, I really wanted to compete in the Utility Expert class with my old racing buddy, Chris Robinson. I think the last time we raced together was in a 2014 TORN race. I think I first met and raced with him a decade before then in the old ATVCCS series. I've always looked up to Chris as one of the faster utility class racers. He has a ton of racing experience (including at GNCC races) and success under his belt, so my goal on this day was simply to follow him and maybe pick up a few pointers. Chris races a Canam Renegade 1000r Xxc that is similar to mine.

When it came time for the start of our afternoon race, Chris and I lined up together next to two fast racers in the 40+ Expert class (Matt and Cory). At that point, Matt, Chris, and I had all competed in the morning ATV race and only Cory had fresh legs. Oddly enough, Matt generously loaned one of his race quads to Cory so that he could compete against Matt in this race. Only Matt would do such a kind and stupid thing! LOL Matt loves to race more than anyone I know, so I wasn't surprised at all by his generosity.

When the flag was raised, I was on the far left side of the starting line and got off to a slow start. Cory won the holeshot, followed closely by Matt, Chris, and finally me in last position.

After maneuvering through the first few turns next to the parking lot, the course ran straight over a whooped out, sandy section. I watched Chris run up the left side of the trail and quickly pass Matt. Chris nailed the throttle and skimmed over the top of each bump like a pro! It was impressive to watch. Soon thereafter, Chris passed Cory and was leading the pack as we made our way around the track for Lap 1.

Chris Robinson taking a commanding lead in the Utility Expert ATV class of Round 4. Photo courtesy of Davey Kroll with DK28 Photography.

After a quarter-mile or so, I found myself all alone as the three guys who started with me quickly checked out. Suddenly, I saw Cory ahead in the woods. He was stopped on the track and Matt was sitting next to him. Cory's quad had stalled, and Matt was helping to get it re-started. I passed both and proceeded to chase Chris, who was long gone at that point.

A few laps later, two of the faster racers from the Open B class (Jered Hunt and Dayton Porter) closed in on me as I raced through the small, square pasture area with zig-zag turns. I kept an eye on them and planned to pull over as soon as they reached my rear bumper. That finally happened in the super tight woods just after the pasture. I pulled to the left about 10 yards before reaching the super tight turn that sometimes caused me to backup. Then I watched in amazement as the two sport quads took a different line to the right side. They both pushed past a few small limbs sticking out next to a small tree and proceeded down a clear path with a smooth, easy right turn at the end instead of the more difficult line on the left that occasionally caused me to back up during in the morning race and the first half of this race. Doh!

This was a good reminder to always look out for alternate lines that may be quicker or easier.

At the end of Lap 4, Chad (a TX4 staffer and fellow SxS racer) mentioned that he saw Chris pull off the trail just past the scoring chute and I still might have a chance to win if I kept going. That lit a fire in me, and I put the hammer down for the final lap.

Later, I found out that Chris was totally exhausted and pulled over to catch his breath. Once he had his helmet off, he decided he had enough fun for the day and thought he already completed enough laps to grab the win anyway. Fortunately for me, he was mistaken about his number of completed laps. Despite running two minutes slower per lap than Chris, I grabbed the win simply because I finished one more lap than he did. As I've said many times before, it is better to be lucky than good. LOL But seriously, it was great fun to race with Chris again, and I hoped to do it again in the near future.

SATURDAY NIGHT:

I'm always grateful when a food vendor shows up at the TX4 races because that means I don't have to resort to peanut butter and crackers for my meals. A food vendor called Turkey Leg Nation catered this event, and the husband-wife cooking team were a big hit with the racers and spectators alike. I loved their brisket sandwich and sausage wrap too. I noticed many others enjoying their Brisket Mac-N-Cheese dish. It was good stuff!

Around 6:30 p.m., Terry casually led a dozen off-road vehicles around the SxS track for another relaxing poker run. With Halloween just two days away, some of the racer's kids were dressed in costumes, and candy was passed around. There were lots of laughs and cold refreshments enjoyed by all as we stopped at different points along the SxS course to draw cards. For a while, I thought I might have the winning hand as I picked up three spades in a row before eventually ending up with four spades and one club. So much for a flush. In the end, Jered Hunt won the $150 pot and the rest went to the series.

I found out later that Jered kept his $20 entry fee and donated the rest to the series. How cool is that? As usual, the poker run was great fun, and I looked forward to the next one in November.

By 8 p.m., I was completely exhausted and set up my bed on the open trailer directly under the canopy. I purposely camped out near the entrance and away from the rest of the campers so as to avoid the noise coming from generators and late-night party animals. Unfortunately, my plans for a peaceful night's rest were spoiled by a group of playful kids who were having the time of their lives running up and down the main road on a small side-by-side. I didn't think much of it because I figured they would eventually get bored of buzzing back and forth along the same path. Thirty minutes passed and they were still at it. One hour went by, and their screams of joy only grew louder. Ugh. At 9:30 p.m., I started to pull my hair out as any hope of getting to sleep soon was dashed. Finally at 10 p.m., the kiddos gave their SxS a break, and I hit the hay.

By the time I climbed into bed, the temps had dropped significantly. I brought a blanket, but it wasn't enough to keep me warm when the temps dipped into the low 50s in the wee hours of the night. I ended up wearing my fleece jacket just to keep from shivering. Around 7:30a.m., I awoke to a gorgeous sunrise and enjoyed warm breakfast tacos from Turkey Leg Nation.

SCHEDULE:

The long break between the Saturday night poker run and the Sunday morning SxS practice gave me plenty of time to think. During this quiet time, it occurred to me how different it is to race both an ATV and SxS with TX4 as compared to the simpler routine of just racing a SxS with the previous series. In the old days, my one-day event included waking up before dawn, driving three hours to the track, practicing, racing, attending the podium ceremony (if I was lucky), and then getting home after dark. By comparison, here's my schedule from a typical TX4 weekend:

SATURDAY SCHEDULE

6:30 a.m. – leave home
10:00 a.m. – ATV inspection
10:15 a.m. – ATV practice
11:30 a.m. – morning ATV race
1:00 p.m. – afternoon ATV race
4:15 p.m. – ATV podium
5:00 p.m. – setup primitive campsite
6:30 p.m. – Poker Run

SUNDAY SCHEDULE

10:00 a.m. – SxS practice
12:30 p.m. – SxS race
2:30 p.m. – pack up campsite
3:30 p.m. – SxS podium
7:30 p.m. – get home

As you can see, TX4 racing includes non-stop activities and leaves me 100 percent exhausted come Sunday night. But it's totally worth it, and I'm always looking forward to doing it again soon!

SxS PRACTICE:

At 10 a.m., the SxSs had a parade lap only (no practice lap) led by Terry. Afterwards, I went back to the truck to top off the fuel, clean the air filter, and check tire pressure. After chatting it up with Phil and his co-pilot, Nick Secrest, who were parked next to me, I suited up and headed to the starting line.

Here I am racing in the Turbo SxS class at Powell Ranch 2.0 / Photo courtesy of Jodi Roush.

SxS RACE:

At 12:30 p.m., Cory called the SxS racers to the starting line for a short rider's meeting. Then Cory lined up the one Pro SxS racer on the front row and the three Turbo SxS competitors on the second row. The remaining seven racers in the naturally aspirated SxS class were split into two separate rows.

After Terry (the sole Pro SxS racer) took off, I pulled Big Blue to the left side of the starting line. To my right were Phil and his co-pilot, Nick, plus John. I said a quick prayer for the safety of all racers, and then it was time to focus on the starting flag.

The flag went up, and off we went. John and Phil got a quick jump off the line, and I found myself behind both as we made our way around Turn Number 1. John grabbed the holeshot and Phil and Nick were hot on John's heels. I tried to keep up, but both SxSs checked out on me within a quarter-mile. Ugh.

As the race continued, I held a consistent pace with an average of 9 minutes and 45 seconds per lap. Up ahead, John and Phil were locked in a tight battle for first and second position. For the first three laps, both were running 9 minutes per lap and putting some good distance on me.

Near the beginning of Lap 4, I briefly saw a SxS parked a few feet away from the right side of the course. It looked like John's RZR Turbo, but I wasn't sure.

It was also during Lap 4 that Sean B. and Chad (both from the Naturally-aspirated SxS class) caught up to me. So I pulled over and let them pass. I followed Chad for the rest of the lap and stayed right on his bumper. I found out later that he never saw me pull over and didn't realize I was right behind him for most of that lap. As we slowly rolled through the scoring chute, Chad finally noticed me and picked up the pace. Soon, he checked out on me. From that point on, I was running my own race again.

Near the beginning of Lap 5, I slowed just enough to confirm that the disabled Side-by-Side parked next to the course was indeed John's. I later found out that his tie rod failed, causing his front two wheels to point towards each other. With him out, that meant I moved up to second position. Woo hoo! Now I had my sights set on Phil and Nick somewhere up ahead.

Speaking of Phil, he started feeling queasy during Lap 5 and slowed down to my pace. At some point, things went downhill fast for him as his body said, "no, thanks!" to the Red Bull he consumed just before the race began. Phil started puking and the vomit quickly filled up the front of his helmet and spilled onto the front of his fire-proof racing suit. Let's hope his suit was stain-proof too. Poor guy!

Things got interesting again near the end of Lap 6. As I ran through the last section of woods, I saw three white cows on the loose, and they were walking in my direction. Yikes! Then I followed the course to my right and headed into the last open section near the entrance to the property. I still had one final lap to complete and was concerned for the safety of all racers, including myself. A minute later, I told Cory about the loose cattle as I went through the scoring chute. He said they've been out the entire weekend, and it would be okay.

On my seventh and final lap, I was relieved to see that the cows were no longer next to the fence where I saw them on the previous lap. Then I made the hard right turn into the woods and suddenly saw one of the white cows munching on a bush right in front of me. DANG IT! I slammed on my brakes and quickly steered to the right. Mr. Cow was startled and walked directly into my path. Luckily, I stopped before turning him into a steak dinner. Then he moved out of the way, and I was able to continue.

Despite getting sick near the end of the race, Phil finished all seven laps and held onto the lead. Mucho congrats to Phil and Nick for taking the win! Later, Phil stood on the podium and joked that he would like to *not thank* Red Bull for the win.

Surprisingly, I reached the podium in all three of my races that weekend, including taking the win in Utility Expert, second place in Turbo SxS, and third in Utility Amateur. Win or lose, I had a blast racing with my TX4 brothers and sisters. With four races of the six races completed thus far, the TX4 series was starting to feel more like a family than a group of strangers who happen to share a common passion for cross-country racing. I was looking forward to seeing everyone again at the next round scheduled for November 19-20.

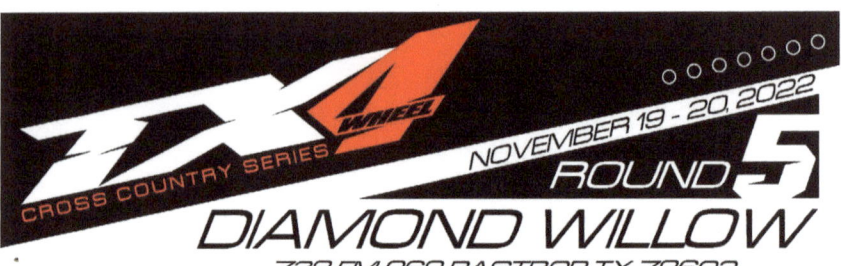

TX4 CROSS COUNTRY SERIES
NOVEMBER 19 - 20, 2022 — ROUND 5
DIAMOND WILLOW
738 FM 969 BASTROP TX 78602

WEEKEND SCHEDULE:

FRIDAY - GATES 2:30 - 11 pm
REGISTRATION 4 - 8 pm

SATURDAY - GATES 7 - 11 pm
REGISTRATION 7 - 6 pm

SUNDAY - GATES 7 - 2 pm
REGISTRATION 7 - 12 pm

ATV RACING
- **8 - 8:30** MINI PRACTICE
- **9am** MINI RACE (30 min)
- **10:15 - 11** ADULT ATV PRACTICE
- **11:30** VINTAGE / OPEN C / UTILITY 40+ AM / BLASTER / ATC / WOMEN (60 min)
- **1 pm** PRO (90 min) OPEN A / OPEN B / 40+ EXPERT / UTILITY EXPERT (70 min)
- **3:00** PIT QUAD LINEUP / SIGHT LAP
- **3:15** PIT QUAD RACE (30 min)
- **4:15** ATV PODIUM (30 min)
- **5:00** POKER RUN / TRACK CRAWL ($20 per hand cash only)

UTV RACING
- **8:30** MINI UTV SIGHT LAP
- **9:00** MINI UTV RACE (30 min)
- **10:00** SIGHT LAP FOR ALL ADULT UTVs
- **10:30** WOMEN / 50+ / 800 / SPORTSMAN BEGINNER RACE (60 min)
- **12:30** PRO / TURBO OPEN / NA OPEN
- **1:40** OPEN CHECKERED FLAG
- **2:00** PRO CHECKERED FLAG
- **2:30** ALL UTV PODIUM

RACE FEES
- **GATE FEE** $10 (UNDER 6 / OVER 60 FREE)
- **CAMPING** $20
- **MEMBERSHIP** $40
- **FULL SIZE ATV** $50
- **PRO ATV** $75
- **MINI ATV** $30
- **FULL SIZE SXS** $90
- **PRO SXS** $180
- **MINI SXS** $40

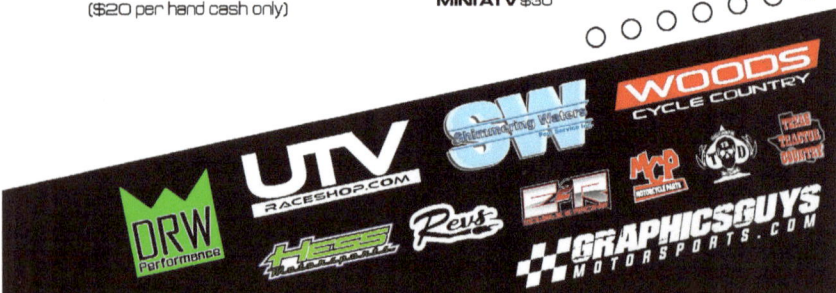

CHAPTER 6:
Diamond Willow 2.0

Round 5 of the TX4 Cross-Country Series will go down in history as the event that separated the men from the boys. In this grueling event, 35 ATVs and 16 SxSs (including minis) braved the harsh elements at Diamond Willow Ranch. On Saturday, November 19th, the ATV races were held in sloppy conditions with constant rainfall and 40-degree temps. Racers who were lucky enough to see through their muddy, fogged up goggles struggled just stay on course. Slick conditions caused many competitors to slide into trees, creeks, or other obstacles. These intense conditions reminded ATV racers what "all terrain" truly means. Sunday's weather improved slightly (same cold temps, but no rain), and most of the SxS track was nearly perfect except for a half-dozen muddy sections to maneuver through.

SATURDAY:

At 6:40 a.m., I wiped the sleep from my eyes and hit the road. Two and a half hours later, I arrived at Diamond Willow in Bastrop, Texas. It rained on and off during the long drive, which was a sign of things to come.

TRACK CONDITIONS:

Unlike the warm, dry conditions that TX4 enjoyed on this property in April, this weekend's event was the exact opposite. This time, the heavens opened up and drenched the area with soaking rain all day Saturday and both days saw chilly temperatures. The poor conditions caused lousy traction, visibility problems, and comfort issues (keeping the body warm and dry).

To stay warm and dry, the experienced racers came prepared. My old racing buddy, Matt Horton, wore a black trash bag under his chest protector to keep the rain from soaking through to his jersey. His ingenious solution was lighter and more economic than mine, which consisted of a last-minute shopping trip to purchase a water-resistant jacket and pants. Also, some racers wore latex gloves under their regular gloves to keep their hands from getting wet. Wish I had thought of that!

The ATV and SxS tracks included 5.8 miles of twisty trails through the woods, sweeping turns around tall trees in wide, bumpy pastures, plus a handful of sloppy creek crossings. One of the few differences between these courses was that the quad track ran along the bottom of a long creek for about 100 yards and then climbed out via a muddy embankment on the left side, whereas the SxS track ran beside the creek, then suddenly turned left at a 90-degree angle to cross the 10-foot deep creek. After climbing out of the creek on the other side, the course made a hard right and continued running along the bank on that side of the creek. Both courses were a blast. Can I get a Yee-haw?

ATV PRACTICE:

On Saturday morning, a large group of clean ATV racers gathered around the starting line for a parade lap and practice session. Weather conditions were cold, wet, and miserable on the outside, but everyone (including me) was beaming on the inside in anticipation of the crazy fun times about to go down.

As the parade lap began, I noticed the following things about the course. First, it seemed long at 5.8 miles in total length according to the Couch Rocket's odometer. Second, the muddy trails were so slimy in places that I occasionally slid off course despite the fact that 4-wheel drive was engaged. Third, my hands and feet were absolutely freezing! I wore an old pair of shoes and gloves because I didn't want to get my good gear wet before the race. Last, I noticed several spots in the woods with large stumps. One of the TX4 staffers and a fellow SxS racer, Bill Deck, recently painted the hidden ones with bright orange paint to alert racers (more on this later).

If you look closely, you can see the orange-painted stump in this view of the muddy race course / Photo courtesy of Mike Kowis.

ATV RACE:

A few minutes before the 11:30 a.m. start, I watched as 20 quads in the parking lot headed towards the starting line. But I wasn't quite ready to go. I quickly added two bottles of water to my camelback, threw on the rest of my gear, and headed to the starting line. Just as I pulled away from my truck, I heard the Open C racers fire up and roar off the line. Luckily, the Utility Amateur class started after all other classes (Open C, Blasters, Vintage, 40+ Amateurs, and Trikes) on this day, so I still had a few minutes to spare.

I lined up in the last row with two other utility quad racers on my right side. One of the regular racers (Gene) was supposed to join us, but his quad was having mechanical problems that day. I introduced myself to newbie racers, Craig King and Josh Horton, and wished them good luck. Both competitors had older, midsized utility quads. Obviously, there was a big difference between their smaller, stock-looking quads and the Couch Rocket. One of the guys looked over at my ATV and jokingly said, "1000ccs… I think that's cheating!" LOL

When the green flag went up, I hit the go button and grabbed a handful of throttle. I easily won the holeshot and set my sights on running a "clean" race in not-so-clean conditions.

Near the first mile, the course ran alongside a tree-lined creek and crisscrossed it several times. Some of these crossings were covered in thick, slimy mud. At one point, I made a left turn down into the creek bottom and then tried to continue turning left as I climbed out on the other side. Unfortunately, my front wheels didn't grab despite being in 4-wheel drive, and I accidentally slammed into several low-hanging tree limbs. Ouchie!

After a quick inspection, I realized the Couch Rocket was unharmed. So, I pointed the front tires in the right direction, mashed the throttle, and climbed the rest of the way out of the muddy creek. Hip, hip, hooray! As the race continued, I slid off the course a few more times. Luckily, the Couch Rocket avoided serious damage each time, and I pushed forward.

The rain continued to fall on and off during the race, which only added to the cold, miserable racing conditions. But everyone on the course that day, including myself, put on a brave face and made the best of it. We weren't going to let a little bad weather stop us from having fun.

On the third lap, I came around a sharp corner in the woods and sped up quickly as I entered a fast, straight section. Near the end of that run, I chopped the throttle to slow down for the hard, right-hand turn coming up soon. Despite letting off the thumb throttle, my engine was still revving high and the Couch Rocket wasn't slowing a bit. Yikes! I mashed the front and rear brakes, but that only slowed me down from 40-something mph to approximately 30 mph. I was quickly running out of real estate before the next turn, so I started to freak out. I pressed and released the throttle quickly to see if it would unstick the throttle. After a half-dozen tries, the engine revs finally dropped and I was able to slow down right before the next turn. What a relief!

After one hour and ten minutes on the sloppy course, I completed my final lap and took the win. The official results indicated that I completed four laps with an average lap time of 17 and one-half minutes. This equates to 20 mph on average, which is a bit off my typical pace. The two challenges that slowed me down the most were trying to see through mud-covered goggles and staying on the slippery course.

Immediately after passing the checkered flag, I made a quick run to the truck to prepare for the next race starting at 1:30 p.m. I topped off the fuel tank, added water to my camelback, and grabbed dry gloves and more tear-offs for my goggles. Next, I made my way back to the starting line and chatted with my friend, Matt Horton, about the crazy racing conditions we just experienced.

Due to the inclement weather, TX4 officials allowed non-Pro racers in the 1:30 p.m. race to decide whether to compete for 60 minutes minimum instead of the usual 70 minutes. We agreed that 60 was plenty. However, Matt and I technically only needed to complete one lap each to earn season points because we were the only competitor in our respective classes. So "one and done" was my initial plan.

When the green flag came out, Matt and I were lined up together – just to make the start more interesting. I barely grabbed the holeshot, but immediately pulled over to let Matt take the lead. Even if I could keep up with Matt's sport quad (which I can't), there would be no benefit in trying to beat him because we are in different classes. So, I followed Matt from a distance and focused on finishing a lap or two. After slipping and sliding for two laps, I called it a day and headed back to the truck. Wearing cold, muddy clothes for the last few hours was starting to annoy me. I wanted nothing more than to change into clean, dry clothes and grab a bite to eat from the food truck. I didn't get the vendor's name, but their "TX4 Cheeseburger" topped with chopped brisket hit the spot. Mmmm!

The Couch Rocket and me posing for a selfie after two muddy races in Round 5. Photo courtesy of Mike Kowis.

SATURDAY NIGHT:

Due to the lousy weather, the ATV podium ceremony and poker run were both cancelled. After my second race, Cory and his cousin, Craig Smith, each generously offered to let me crash in their RVs that night rather than roughing it outdoors like I normally do. I thanked them both, but declined because I had anticipated the poor weather and already booked a hotel room in the nearby town of Bastrop.

Taking a hot shower and sleeping in a warm bed that evening felt like Heaven compared to my usual routine. I actually got a full night's rest on Saturday night, which never happens when I sleep at the track under a canopy. Despite this luxurious experience, I planned to return to my usual camping routine at the next race, assuming the weather cooperates. I don't have a good reason for primitive camping other than I'm cheap like that. Plus, camping outdoors usually makes for a good story. LOL

SxS PRACTICE:

On Sunday morning, I ate a hot breakfast at the hotel and then made my way back to the track around 9 a.m. I arrived in time to chat with my fellow SxS racers, including Phil and his new co-pilot Landon Smith. Phil would be my only competition on Sunday because John made previously planned a trip to the Little Sahara State Park. I couldn't blame him for doing that because Cash and I thoroughly enjoyed riding there last June.

When the single parade lap started at 10:30 a.m., I was busy taking pics and joking around with Phil and Landon. By the time I got my helmet on and strapped into Big Blue, I was the last SxS to leave the starting area.

(from left to right) Landon Smith, Phil Waggoner, and me joking around before the SxS parade lap at Round 5 / Photo courtesy of Mike Kowis.

As I made my way around the course, I noticed many of Saturday's muddy spots were gone. However, a handful of extremely slippery spots remained to challenge the SxS racers.

Being the last one in the parade lap, I took my time and occasionally stopped to take pics of the course. Except for the few sloppy places mentioned above, most of the track was in excellent racing condition. Afterwards, I went back to my truck so I could prep Big Blue and then waited for my 1 p.m. race.

While waiting at my truck, I saw a few smiling faces approach me. Randy Lewis came all the way from California to meet me and watch me race. He brought along his two grandkids too. I have been in contact with Randy for a few years because he has a fascinating hobby called "track chasing." In a nutshell, Randy travels all over the world to watch live racing events like the SxS races offered by TX4. I tried to meet up with him a few years ago at one of the SxS races offered by the former series, but I had mechanical problems that weekend and couldn't make it. Ironically, that was the first SxS race that I missed in three years. Ugh. Luckily, it worked out this time, and I was able to meet Randy in person. He took pics and video during my SxS race and congratulated me afterwards. He later shared this experience and recordings via his newsletter and website. If interested, check out www.randylewis.org.

SxS RACE:

When 1 p.m. rolled around, Cory held the rider's meeting. After explaining the general rules, he walked around the cars to check for working chase lights, and then it was go time.

Next, Cory lined up three Pro SxS competitors on the front row, two Turbo SxS racers on the second row, and the remaining six racers in the naturally aspirated class on the last row.

After the Pros took off, I pulled Big Blue to the left side of the starting line and Phil and Landon were on my immediate right. Now we were ready to rock!

Soon, the flag went up and off we went. Big Blue's engine quickly started, and I left the line just a milli-second faster than Phil. I took the holeshot and proceeded to put the hammer down. Yippee!

As I made my way through the first mile of track, I noticed Phil and Landon were hot on my tail. So, I kept the pedal pushed to the floor as much as I dared. The pace was frantic, and the course felt like riding a bucking bronco. Big Blue fell into deep ruts, rode up on two wheels around sharp turns, bounced all over the track in the bumpy pasture areas, slammed into low-hanging tree limbs, all of which caused me to hang on for dear life. All the while, Phil and Landon were looming in my rearview mirror and itching to take over the lead. My job was to not let that happen.

At some point during the first few laps, I ran underneath one of the tall trees in the open pasture and collided with a big tree limb. As I pushed through the turn, it suddenly snapped backwards and slammed into Phil's car right behind me. He saw it coming and yelled at Landon to look out! LOL Luckily, no one was hurt, and we had a good laugh about it after the race.

A mile into Lap 1, Phil and I approached a muddy creek crossing. As I made a sharp left into the creek bottom, I tried to hug the tree line on the left so as to prevent Phil from passing me on the inside. But as I exited that turn, the trail suddenly made a hard right turn that goes uphill. The entire face of the hill was a muddy mess. I tried to make the hard right turn, but my front wheels didn't get traction causing me to swing wide around that turn. Wasting no time, Phil seized the opportunity to take the inside line around that turn and take the lead from me. Dang it!

From that point, I tried to follow close, but not so close that Phil would throw mud on my goggles or into my radiator - and risk overheating Big Blue. As we pressed on, the track wound back and forth through the open pasture and finally entered the woods on the backside of the property. Once in the woods, I quickly lost sight of Phil and Landon.

A minute later, I saw Phil's car pulled off to the right side of the trail. He accidentally slid past a slippery turn and had to back up. Just as I approached him, I heard him griding gears in an attempt to quickly back up. I was able to (barely) squeeze between his car on the right and the trees on the left and then took over the lead again. Woo hoo!

I finished the first and second laps with Phil and Landon hot on my heals. I pushed myself as hard as Big Blue could go. Honestly, this pace was faster than I'd raced all season and it was thrilling! I kept thinking if I keep up this pace, I might hit a tree or have a mechanical issue on my 5-year-old race buggy. But I kept going for two reasons: it was a total blast, and I wanted to see what would happen.

One mile into Lap 3, we approached the same slippery S curve where Phil passed me on Lap 1. I was careful to hug the inside line around the first turn and then attempted to hug the inside line around the next turn that points uphill. Suddenly, my front wheels slid again and Phil passed me in the exact same spot as Lap 1. Doh!

While I tried my best to keep up with Phil, he soon checked out and disappeared by the time we entered the wooded section near the back of the property. At that point, I was determined to keep up my pace and see if could eventually catch him.

As I made my way through the woods, I saw one of the painted stumps on the right side of the trail and tried to avoid it. Suddenly, I heard a loud "BANG" from the right side and instantly knew I nailed the stump. Oh, crap! I kept going and hoped for the best. As I got further down the trail, I could tell something was off. The steering seemed out-of-whack, and the buggy was hard to control. Soon, I entered the scoring chute and Cory yelled at me that my right front tire was nearly flat. That was not what I wanted to hear, but it wasn't a surprise given how poorly it handled. I pulled off to the side and Cory said he'd check to see how much time was left in the race. He soon came back and let me know there was only 18 minutes to go. That meant I'd get season points if I decided to quit the race now. (TX4 rules state that each racer must complete at least half the number of laps as the first place finisher in your class to receive season points) Cory also mentioned that Phil was still racing, but he was nursing a flat rear tire. I said thanks and then headed back to my truck to see if I could air up the tire. I broke out the bicycle pump and hit it 70 times as fast as I could. By the time the tire seemed to be back to almost normal size, I was completely out of breath! LOL

*Giving a thumbs down for the punctured front tire in Round 5.
Photo courtesy of Mike Kowis.*

I hopped back in and headed back to the scoring chute area to begin my Lap 4. I realized there was no chance of catching Phil and Landon if their car was in decent condition. However, I thought maybe I could catch them if they slow way down to nurse their car around the track with the flat rear tire.

As I made my way around Lap 4, I could tell that the front right tire was not holding air again. It was obvious by the way Big Blue handled sharp turns and bumps. What I didn't know at the time was that the stump left a two-inch slit in the sidewall and there was no way to stop the leak. In any case, I chose to press onward and see what happened.

Midway through Lap 4, I noticed Phil's car parked on the right side of the trail and no one was inside. I was shocked. What happened to his car and where did the occupants go?

A few turns later, I saw both guys walking back towards the front of the property and they waved as I passed them. Holy Toledo! I just re-took the lead. I found out later that Phil slid into a tree that completely took out his entire right front wheel. Apparently, he forgot that 3-wheelers only race on Saturday - not Sunday! LOL

Now all I needed to do was complete Lap 4 to win the race. So, I kept going and prayed that Big Blue would make it back to the scoring chute. When I finally got there, I was so relieved!

Randy stopped by afterwards to ask how I finished. I explained what happened and told him the moral is never give up. Good things happen if you keep trying and today was the perfect example of that. Racing with Phil and Landon on this challenging course was the most exciting race of the season for me thus far, and I hoped to do it again soon. This race was one for the history books!

Smiling after a grueling, come-from-behind win at Round 5 / Photo courtesy of Mike Kowis.

When the official results were posted, I took first place in all three of my races that weekend and had a ball doing it. It was such an adventure racing in the crazy weather with my fellow racers, and I couldn't wait for the final round scheduled for December.

TX4 CROSS COUNTRY SERIES
DECEMBER 17-18, 2022 — ROUND 6
LET'S RIDE RANCH
1210 CR205B BUCKHOLTS, TX 76518

WEEKEND SCHEDULE:

FRIDAY - GATES 2:30 - 11 pm
REGISTRATION 4 - 8 pm
SATURDAY - GATES 7 - 11 pm
REGISTRATION 7 - 6 pm

SUNDAY - GATES 7 - 2 pm
REGISTRATION 7 - 12 pm

ATV RACING

8 - 8:30 MINI PRACTICE
9 am MINI RACE (30 min)
10:15 - 11 ADULT ATV PRACTICE
11:30 VINTAGE / OPEN C / UTILITY 40+ AM / BLASTER / ATC / WOMEN (60 min)
1 pm PRO (90 min)
OPEN A / OPEN B / 40+ EXPERT / UTILITY EXPERT (70 min)
3:00 PIT QUAD LINEUP / SIGHT LAP
3:15 PIT QUAD RACE (30 min)
4:15 ATV PODIUM (30 min)
5:00 POKER RUN / TRACK CRAWL ($20 per hand cash only)

UTV RACING

8:30 MINI UTV SIGHT LAP
9:00 MINI UTV RACE (30 min)
10:00 SIGHT LAP FOR ALL ADULT UTVs
10:30 WOMEN / 50+ / 800 / SPORTSMAN BEGINNER RACE (60 min)
12:30 PRO / TURBO OPEN / NA OPEN
1:40 OPEN CHECKERED FLAG
2:00 PRO CHECKERED FLAG
2:30 ALL UTV PODIUM

RACE FEES

GATE FEE $10
UNDER 8 / OVER 60 FREE
CAMPING $20
MEMBERSHIP $40
FULL SIZE ATV $50
PRO ATV $75
MINI ATV $30

FULL SIZE SXS $90
PRO SXS $180
MINI SXS $40

CHAPTER 7:
Let's Ride Ranch

Before the crack of dawn on December 17th, Cash and I loaded up Big Blue and the Couch Rocket and began our 3-hour drive to Let's Ride Ranch in Buckholts, Texas for the last round of the 2022 TX4 cross-country series. Before this event, I'd only been to this property once for the last race of the former SxS series (held one year earlier). Big Blue broke down in the middle of that race, so I was hoping for better results this time. Turnout for this final round was solid with 40 ATVs and 20 side-by-sides competing, including minis.

Here I am launching the Couch Rocket off a small jump in Round 6.
Photo courtesy of Jodi Roush.

TRACK CONDITIONS:

At race time, the weather was chilly, but nice (mid-50s and partly sunny). The track was mostly dry, except for a few muddy creek crossings here and there. Thankfully, the dust wasn't bad at all.

The ATV and SxS courses had a similar layout except for different wooded sections here and there. Both tracks measured 4.4 miles according to my speedo. Overall, the track was fast and flowed well. But it could also be rough in some sections, especially the woods (which had plenty of tire hazards) and also in the open fields (which included several zig-zag turns). The course also crossed in and out of dry creeks in many places.

ATV PRACTICE:

On Saturday morning, ATV racers met up with Zach for tech inspection and then headed to the starting line for practice at 10:15 a.m.

When the first practice lap began, I joined the pack of eager ATV racers, and we slowly made our way past the first (right hand) turn around a small tree. Suddenly, a blue sport quad in front of me spun his rear tires around that turn, caught traction on his left tires and rolled over. He immediately hopped up on both feet as if to say, "yeah, I meant to do that!" LOL He appeared uninjured and climbed back on his quad to continue the practice lap. That little incident was a good reminder of why we wear so much safety gear!

MORNING ATV RACE:

On that day, the Utility Amateur ATV class had five competitors. Joining me once again was Sean Burnett on his classic "Bomb-a-deer" 400, which is so old it probably belongs in a museum. Also in attendance was Sean's fearless brother Gene riding atop the lean, mean, fighting machine Kymco 500. John showed up with a different machine than normal. This time, his mighty steed was a camouflaged 2016 Renegade 1000r with green accents. Chris Cluck joined the fun again with his CFMoto 400. You can't miss his quad because his bright orange fenders stand out from all the others. Together, the five of us (mostly dressed in jeans and work boots) looked less like serious quad racers and more like the Village People (in case you didn't know, that music group was a popular 1970s band who dressed up in silly costumes). Regardless of how we looked, we had one heck of a time!

Utility Amateur ATV class lined up for the start of Round 6. Photo courtesy of Jodi Roush.

When our class pulled up to the starting line, I lined up in the middle with John on my immediate right and Sean B. on my immediate left. The first right-hand turn was approximately 60-feet ahead.

As the flagman pointed to me, I nodded my head to indicate I was ready and then focused my attention on the green flag in his hand. As our class took off, I noticed John on my right side pulled a monster wheelie and continued to ride it out. I let off the gas because you never know where someone might come down from a wheelie (obviously, it's impossible to steer with the front tires in the air). When John finally touched down on all four wheels, he was leading the pack and grabbed the holeshot. Hot on John's heals were Gene,

Sean, me, and finally Chris. Taking 4th position around Turn Number 1 was a lousy way to start, so I had my work cut out for me if I was going to get on the podium.

After we raced along the course next to the creek, I slid around the muddy turn near the end of the creek and then headed towards the "golf course" pasture area. I grabbed a handful of throttle and passed Sean just before the sweeping right-hand turn. A half-dozen turns later, we entered the next pasture area where I passed Gene and grabbed second position. Yee-haw! Now I'm back in the hunt.

As I entered the next pasture area, I saw John ahead and counted his lead at approximately 10 seconds. Then I kept my head down and pushed forward to see if I could close the gap.

Halfway around the course, the track ran back and forth through a deep, dry creek crossing with cactus on both sides of the trail. Then it popped out near the backside of the property. Next, racers ran up a small hill, made a hard left turn and descended towards the fence line at the bottom. Just before reaching the barbed wire fence, the track ran through a pile of ashes from an old burn pile (not to be mistaken for the ashes of my failed GNCC racing career!) and then continues past the entrance to the access tunnel that I previously mentioned before finally reaching the last big pasture. Here, racers ran parallel to the highway for a half-mile before turning into an open gate and heading towards a small section of woods adjacent to the scoring chute/starting line area.

The second half of the race was mostly uneventful except for passing a few of the slower racers from other classes and getting lapped by faster racers in the Pro ATV and other classes. For the first three laps, John outpaced me by 30 seconds to 1 minute per lap before he finally slowed way down during his last two laps. For the latter part of the race, I began to catch up. John crossed the finish line just 20 seconds ahead of me. Doh!

As I pulled into the scoring chute at the end of Lap 5, I was exhausted and relieved to see Chad waving the checkered flag. Big congrats to John for taking the win! I finished in second place, Gene took third, followed by Chris in fourth, and finally Sean – who pulled out after Lap 1.

AFTERNOON ATV RACE:

Surprisingly, I had some energy left after the morning race. So, I registered for the Utility Expert class in the afternoon ATV race. I knew that I would be the only person in this class that day, but I wanted to race anyway to get season points in that class.

As usual, they let me start on the same line as the faster racers in the 40+ Expert class to make things interesting. On this day, there were three guys from that class (Cory, Matt, and Mike Walker) on the line next to me. When the flag came up, I was last around the first turn and stayed in hot pursuit as long as I could. Despite my best efforts, they checked out on me within a half-mile.

Because I was the only competitor in the Utility Expert class, I only needed to complete one lap to receive season points. However, I decided to run the full 70 minutes because I was having too much fun to quit early. Afterwards, I was completely exhausted as I logged in 50 miles on my quad that day, including both races and practice laps. Now that's what I call getting my money's worth!

SATURDAY NIGHT:

Around 5 p.m., Terry slowly led a dozen side-by-sides and ATVs around the SxS track for the last poker run of the year. For this event, Cash took the driver's seat and I hopped into the co-pilot seat with a cold beverage or two. Even though Cash and I never end up with the winning hand, the poker run has become one of my favorite parts of the TX4 weekend.

Afterwards, Cash and I returned to the truck to load up. Instead of primitive camping at the track like we usually did, we opted to grab a local hotel room just 10 minutes up the road. Turns out that was the right call because the temps dipped down to 29 degrees overnight, and we found a layer of frost all over the truck in the morning. Brrr!

SxS PRACTICE:

On Sunday morning at 10 a.m., the SxSs lined up on the starting line for the parade lap.

After practice, Cash and I went back to the truck to top off the fuel and check tire pressure. Big Blue was wearing new shoes for this race after suffering a front tire blowout near the end of the last race. Instead of replacing the Dirt Commanders with the same ones, I opted to try a set of Dirt Commander 2.0 tires. The new version has the same tread pattern, but with beefier, squared side walls and it is radial instead of bias ply. The 2.0 version weighs a bit more than the original version, but should be more puncture resistant. This race was my first opportunity to try the new tires, and I was anxious to see if I liked them more than the original version. (more on this later)

Let's Ride Ranch normally operates as an off-road park and is divided by a highway that cuts through the middle. Under the highway is a tunnel that allows off-road vehicles to access both sides of the park. The TX4 races were held on only one side of the park, so I had not yet seen the other side. After the parade lap, I decided to ride my quad through the tunnel to explore the other side. Turns out that side is smaller, but had lots of wooded trails. Cash and I hoped to return someday to ride the entire park for fun.

SxS RACE:

When it came time to start the SxS races, four Pro SxS racers lined up on the front row, five Turbo SxS racers gathered on the second row, and seven Naturally-Aspirated SxS class made up the last two rows.

This SxS race was particularly exciting because both the Turbo and Naturally-Aspirated classes had a tight points race for the leader. In the Turbo SxS class,

Phil and I were nearly tied in season points going into this race. That meant the 2022 Championship came down to this final race! Phil and his co-pilot Landon worked feverishly over the last few days to put their RZR Turbo back together after hitting a tree in the final lap of the last race. I was so glad he could make it to this event so we could find out who would be crowned "Season Champ" and who would be called "Season Chump!"

After the Pro SxS class took off, I pulled Big Blue to the middle of the starting line. From left to right, the line-up was Phil and his co-pilot Landon, a TX4 newbie and past TORN Turbo SxS Champ named Justin Berube, me and Cash, Dwayne Sanders, and John. Cash and I said a quick prayer, and it was finally go time. Let the games begin!

Cory waved the green flag and off we went. John had a great start and quickly took the inside line to the first turn. John won the holeshot with Justin right on his heels. Next, Phil and I rounded the first turn together with Phil just inches ahead of me. Finally, Dwayne came around Turn Number 1 in last position, which is exactly what he said he'd do before the race because he knew Phil and I were in a tight points race.

As we moved closer to the second (left-hand) turn, Phil had the inside line. So, I backed off and took my place immediately behind his rear bumper. I wasn't worried about starting off in fourth position because my only goal was to beat Phil and take home the season championship. Halfway through Lap 1, we saw Justin pulled over to the side of the course, which meant Phil and I moved up to second and third positions, respectively. Cash and I kept Phil's car within eye-sight for the entire first lap. In fact, we rolled through the scoring chute at the end of Lap 1 only 10 seconds behind Phil and Landon. What an exciting way to start the race!

In the middle of Lap 2, disaster struck! Just past the first set of woods, the track ran along the tree line and then made a hard right-hand turn down into a deep, dry creek crossing. As Big Blue hit the bottom of the crossing, I heard a loud bang and immediately thought, "Oh crapola!" I hoped nothing broke. I continued on and the car felt okay at first. But a half-mile down the track, I could tell that Big Blue didn't handle turns as well as normal. My gut told me that I had a flat tire, but I wasn't sure which one.

*Cash and me piloting Big Blue in Round 6 – before the flat tire!
Photo courtesy of Jodi Roush.*

Then I saw my old racing pal, Collin Huber, parked off to the right side of the trail. Collin raced his quad the day before, but was there on Sunday just to watch the SxSs and show his support for TX4. I pulled up alongside him and quickly asked if I had a flat. Collin confirmed that my driver-side rear tire was toast. My heart sunk, and I immediately thought, "Well, there goes my season." There was nothing left to do but slowly finish lap 2 and head back to the trailer with our tails between our legs.

Congrats to John for taking the win in the Turbo SxS class that day. Phil and Landon finished in second and Dwayne S. took the final spot on the podium. Justin and me got a DNF. The final season points for all racers would be calculated by the TX4 staff and announced a few days later. Now it was just a waiting game to see where Cash and I ended up.

CONCLUSION

A few days after Round 6, TX4 staff released the official standings for the Turbo SxS class. I couldn't believe my eyes. I beat Phil by one freakin' point! I had forgotten that TX4 awards five bonus points for perfect attendance and those points were just barely enough to give Cash and me the 2022 Championship in the Turbo SxS class. Woo hoo!

In addition, I also won the 2022 Championships for both the Utility Amateur ATV class and Utility Expert ATV class. To recap, I won three championships in one season – something I never thought I'd do in my lifetime. It was a good year for sure, but mostly I was just grateful that Terry and Cory quickly brought this new series to life and gave off-road enthusiasts the opportunity to continue cross-country racing in the Lone Star State. I don't know what I'd do without TX4.

On the evening of January 21, 2023, Terry and Cory hosted the 2022 TX4 Awards Banquet at a quaint café located directly across the street from the entrance to Rusty's Walnut Creek Ranch. Racers and their families were invited to grab a bite to eat from the tasty food vendor (named "Wat Tha Truck") parked just outside the establishment and then find a spot to sit inside. Cory emceed the festive event while Terry handed out plaques and goodie bags to the winners. It was great fun to hear each winner talk about their 2022 season and give thanks to those who supported them – usually family, friends, sponsors, and our Heavenly Father above – as well as the hard-working TX4 staff for making it all possible. When it was my turn to get on stage, I thanked all of the above (minus sponsors because I don't have any) for their help in winning the 2022 championships in the Utility Amateur ATV class, Utility Expert ATV class, and the Turbo SxS class. Cory and Terry also presented me with a special, one-of-a-kind metal plaque that says "TX4 2022 Triple Champ" along with my name and race number 77. How cool is that? Fun was had by all, and the two-hour event flew by.

(from left to right) Sean Burnett, myself, and John Glover were all smiles as we received our 2022 TX4 season awards for the Utility Amateur ATV class / Photo courtesy of Davey Kroll with DK28 Photography.

*Cash and me counting our spoils at the 2022 TX4 Awards Ceremony.
Photo courtesy of Davey Kroll with DK28 Photography.*

TX4 WHEEL CROSS COUNTRY SERIES
JANUARY 21 - 22, 2023 — ROUND 1

RUSTY'S WALNUT CREEK RANCH
394 PLEASANT CHAPEL RD, CEDAR CREEK, TX 78612

WEEKEND SCHEDULE:

FRIDAY - GATES 2:30 - 11 pm
REGISTRATION 4 - 8 pm

SATURDAY - GATES 7 - 11 pm
REGISTRATION 7 - 6 pm

ATV RACING

8 - 8:30 MINI PRACTICE
9am MINI RACE (30 min)
10 - 10:30 AMATEUR PRACTICE
10:30 - 11 EXPERT / PRO PRACTICE
11:30 VINTAGE / OPEN C / UTILITY 40+ AM / BLASTER / ATC / WOMEN (60 min)
1pm PRO (90 min)
OPEN A / OPEN B / 40+ EXPERT / UTILITY EXPERT (70 min)
3:00 PT QUAD LINEUP / SIGHT LAP
3:15 PT QUAD RACE (30 min)
4:30 2022 AWARDS BANQUET AT CAFE ACROSS THE STREET

SUNDAY - GATES 7 - 2 pm
REGISTRATION 7 - 12 pm

UTV RACING

8:30 MINI UTV SIGHT LAP
9:00 MINI UTV RACE (30 min)
10:00 SIGHT LAP FOR ALL ADULT UTVS
10:30 WOMEN / 50+ / 800 / SPORTSMAN BEGINNER RACE (60 min)
12:30 EXPERT / TURBO OPEN / NA OPEN
1:40 OPEN CHECKERED FLAG
2:00 EXPERT CHECKERED FLAG
2:30 ALL UTV PODIUM

RACE FEES

GATE FEE $10
UNDER 6 / OVER 60 FREE
CAMPING $20
MEMBERSHIP $40
FULL SIZE ATV $50
PRO ATV $75
MINI ATV $30

FULL SIZE UTV $90
EXPERT UTV $180
MINI UTV $40

BONUS CHAPTER:
Cash's First ATV Race!

The 2023 TX4 season started off with a bang as more than 100 entries (59 quads plus 43 side-by-sides) showed up at Rusty's Walnut Creek Ranch in Cedar Creek, Texas to compete on a thrilling track laid out by Terry Deck and company. This January 21st and 22nd event was special for two reasons. First, many folks stuck around on Saturday night to enjoy the 2022 TX4 Awards Banquet described in the last chapter. Second and more important, Cash competed in his first ever ATV race on Saturday – proud dad alert!

TRACK CONDITIONS

Mother nature blessed us this weekend with cool daytime temps in the 50s. Saturday's racers saw lots of cloud cover, but Sunday's racers enjoyed sunny skies. The little bit of rain that fell Saturday morning was just enough the keep the dust down that day, but not enough to prevent dust on some parts of the course during Sunday's events.

Similar to last season, the ATV and SxS courses were similar except for different sections of tight woods here and there. The quad track was 4.7 miles long according to my speedometer and the SxS track was 4.5 miles. Both tracks started in a small open area not far from the back of the large parking lot area. From there, the track ran a half-mile along wide, choppy, and sandy trails before reaching the first tight section of woods. After dodging trees for another mile or so, the course took racers to a big open area under a canopy of tall pecan trees. Here, racers zig-zagged between the trees and then headed back into the tight woods for the final two miles. Overall, the track was fast and flowed well except for a few tight woods that forced racers to check their speed or else risk turning into a 3-wheeler.

ATV PRACTICE:

On Saturday morning, ATV racers met up with Zach for a quick tech inspection and then headed to the starting line for practice beginning at 10 a.m.

As mentioned above, Cash decided to race his 2008 Honda 250ex for the first time ever. So, he joined me for the ATV parade lap and practice laps. A half-mile into the slow-paced site lap, I nearly had a heart attack as I realized my cell phone fell out of my pocket. It was G-O-N-E! Ugh.

I immediately pulled over and asked Cash to help me search for it on the ground. I knew it couldn't be too far away because I last felt it in my pocket only 50 yards behind us. Scott Hardy (TX4's beloved medic and well-known funnyman) plus one of the sweepers immediately stopped to help us search. For the next five stressful minutes, I frantically paced up and down the track in search of my phone and felt absolutely horrible that Cash was missing out on the opportunity to practice for his first race. Suddenly, my son found the phone on the floorboard of the Couch Rocket. It was lying right next to the brake pedal. What a relief! Better yet, we still had time to run a few practice laps. I thanked Cash and Scott, and then we continued our practice laps again.

A few miles up the trail, the course ran straight through the woods for 50 yards, made a 180-degree right turn and then climbed a small hill about 10 feet high. This short climb would have been easy except that it was slightly off-camber (sloping down to the left side) and had a small stump on the top of the hill - on the right side of the trail. As I made the 180-degree turn, I saw a young lady standing next to her sport quad, which was completely sideways at the top of the hill. Cash and I jumped off our ATVs to help straighten out her quad and push it out of the way. Luckily, both the rider and her quad were unharmed, and we proceeded again.

At the end of practice, we headed back to the truck to top off fuel tanks, check tire pressure, and gear up for the 11:30 a.m. race.

Yours truly competing in the Utility Amateur ATV class.
Photo courtesy of Davey Kroll with DK28 Photography.

MORNING ATV RACE:

Joining me in the Utility Amateur class were three returning racers from last season, including John on his Renegade 1000r, Gene on his mighty Kymco 500, and Chris on his bright orange CFMoto 400.

The Utility Amateur class lined up on one of the last few rows, and my son and the rest of the Blaster class were in the back row. I walked back to Cash's row, and we said a quick prayer for the safety of all racers. Then we climbed onto our respective quads and prepared for battle. I'm not gonna lie — I was both excited and nervous about Cash racing for the first time. In fact, it was all I could think about until my class pulled up to the starting line. Then I put my game face on and focused my full attention on the flagman.

I lined up on the far right side of the starting line, and John lined up near the far left side. The last time we raced together, John pulled a big wheelie off the line while I was beside him, and I ended up dropping back because I didn't know where John's quad might come down on all four wheels. This time, I lined up far away from John to avoid that issue.

When the green flag went up, John and I shot off the line first with Gene and Chris leaving the line a split second later. Doing his best Evil Kneivel impression, John pulled another monster wheelie and his Renegade veered to the right side of the track - in my direction. When he finally came down on all four wheels, John won the holeshot with me just off his rear bumper and Gene and Chris in tow.

After Turn Number 1, John flew down the wide, choppy trail, and I tried my best to keep up. A half-mile later, the course ran straight for a few hundred yards and then made a 90-degree left turn at the end. I pushed the Couch Rocket as fast as I dared and stayed just a few seconds behind John. Soon, John and I were both zig-zagging through the tight woods and then weaving in and around the tall pecan trees in the open section. It was there that I could see John up ahead and noticed he was pulling away. So, I kept pushing myself with the hope of somehow catching him.

By the end of Lap 1, I was almost 30 seconds behind John. His lead continued to grow until the final lap when John slowed way down and I finally started to gain back some of the ground I previously lost.

Near the second half of the race, I came around a sweeping right-hand corner near the open area with tall trees and saw Matt Horton standing next to his 3-wheeler… errr, wait. He doesn't race in the Trike class! LOL It turned out that he forgot to torque down the lug nuts, and one rear wheel popped off during the race. It was bad timing too because he was in the lead at that time. But it takes more than a little bad luck to stop Matt. He eventually found a way to get his loose wheel re-installed, and then he finished the race.

When the checkered flag came out, John reached the finish line just 17 seconds ahead of me. Gene finished in third place, and Chris took fourth. Congrats to John for taking the win and to all of us for finishing the race in one piece, which wasn't easy on a course with so many tight woods.

CASH'S FIRST RACE:

Somewhere behind my class, Cash lined up with three other newbie competitors in the Blaster class. Much to his surprise, he had a good start and won the holeshot. Woo hoo! He carried the lead until his quad suddenly stalled and took a few minutes to re-start. In the meantime, two of his competitors passed him, and he dropped back to third position.

After passing through the open section with tall pecan trees, Cash made a hard right turn into the woods with too much speed. He had a split second to decide whether to continue making the turn at high speed and possibly flipping over or staying on all four wheels by hitting a small tree. He chose to re-shape his front bumper (slightly) and luckily that was the only damage suffered, other than his pride.

Lap 2 was trouble-free for Cash, and he made the fastest lap time of everyone in his class at 14 minutes and 42 seconds. Now, he was back in first position and feeling good!

Cash competing in his first ever ATV race – proud dad alert! Photo courtesy of Davey Kroll with DK28 Photography.

However, Lap 3 was frustrating again as his quad stalled a second time within eyeshot of the scoring chute. His Honda didn't just want to re-start and left him stranded. Luckily, Cory came to his rescue and finally got it going again after messing with the choke and fuel petcock. After this mechanical delay, Cash ran a trouble-free Lap 4 and took third place at the checkered flag. It was a close race, and he finished just eight seconds behind second place. He was smiling for the rest of the weekend and was already looking forward to Round 2.

As his father, it was so much fun to see my son racing on the same track as me. And I couldn't be more proud that he won the holeshot and earned a podium finish in his first race despite a few setbacks. That's my boy!

AFTERNOON ATV RACE:

Three Utility Expert class racers lined up on the starting line, including Sean Burnett (who raced last year in the Utility Amateur class), Preston Bissuett (an experienced desert racer, but a newbie to XC racing), and myself. Sean didn't bring his quads to Round 1, so John generously loaned his Renegade 1000r to Sean for this race. That meant I had to compete against the same fast quad twice in one day. Gulp! Preston showed up with his Polaris Outlander 1000, and it looked fully-prepped and ready to race.

I was a bit concerned about my chances in this ATV race because both Sean and Preston had fresh legs while I was competing in my second race of the day. However, I knew Sean was racing a quad that he wasn't familiar with and Preston was brand new to woods racing. So, I didn't count myself out just yet.

On the starting line, I lined up on the far right side with the first left turn about 50 yards ahead. When the green flag popped up, I left the line hard and got to the turn just behind Sean. As we rounded the first turn, Sean took the holeshot, and I fell in line close behind him. Preston was not far behind me.

Compared to the morning race, this one was way more exciting. I rode as close to Sean as I could for the first half mile and watched as he almost blew past the first few turns. He was riding like a wild man, and I wasn't sure if he was going to kill himself or take the overall win… but either way he was going to get there fast! LOL

After the first long straight section, Sean slid past the sharp left-hand turn at the very end, and I took over the lead. From there, I checked out on Sean and ended up with a comfortable, 24-second lead at the end of Lap 1. By the end Lap 2, I had my second wind and was feeling confident with Sean nowhere in sight. Unbeknownst to me, Sean picked up the pace and completed that lap 13 seconds faster than me. In the middle of Lap 3, my plans of cruising to an easy win came crashing down when I noticed Sean catching up to me in the open area under the big pecan trees. Dang it! I pushed the Couch Rocket harder, but Sean kept coming for me.

Not far up the trail, Sean reached my rear bumper and my energy was totally spent. I had nothing left in the tank. I pulled over and let him pass, and then my lap times started dropping despite my best efforts to keep up the pace.

Somewhere behind me, Preston was still hanging in there until his last lap when all heck broke loose! He took a nasty spill from his Outlander on the long, bumpy straight section just before the scoring chute. He hit the ground hard enough to re-shape the side of his helmet (in his words, "it's wall art now"), and he bloodied his nose. Scott checked his vital signs and recommended a trip to the emergency room to be safe. This turned out to be great advice because his injuries were a bit more serious than they first appeared. Funny thing was that Preston showed up at the TX4 Award Banquet before he headed to the hospital so he could accept his third place plaque. What a trooper! Hopefully, he will heal soon and join us again for more fun.

SATURDAY NIGHT:

At 4:30 p.m., Cash and I headed to the 2022 TX4 Awards Banquet at the café located directly across the street from the track's entrance. Immediately afterwards, Cash and I hopped in Big Blue and returned to the parking area where we "enjoyed" another night of primitive camping under the stars. As usual, we set up our sleeping bags and bed cushions on top of our open trailer directly under the canopy. Then we hunkered down for the 40-degree overnight temps. Brrr!

Thankfully, we survived the long, frigid night. The morning greeted us with a beautiful sunrise and the occasional crowing of roosters in the distance. I didn't sleep well and felt a bit groggy. But at least my old bones were well rested.

SxS PARADE LAP:

On Sunday morning at 10 a.m., the SxSs had a parade lap led by Terry. The track looked similar to the ATV course with the exception that the Side-by-Sides ran a different section of tight woods in certain places. We saw a couple of SxSs having trouble getting around some of the extra tight turns and heard about others bumping into the trees in the tight woods. Immediately afterwards, the TX4 crew made a few adjustments to the track, and then everything was ready for action.

After completing the site lap, Cash and I went back to the truck to top off the fuel and check tire pressure on Big Blue. After suiting up for the race, my friend from California (Randy Lewis), showed up and we chatted a bit. I hadn't seen him since he came to watch the TX4 Round 5 race a few months ago. This time, Randy came to watch Cash and me race together, take pics, and earn points toward his favorite hobby, track chasing. Randy is currently ranked number one in the world in this rare and exciting hobby. He also brought me a free T-shirt with his name and logo. Thanks buddy!

John Glover grabbed the holeshot just ahead of Cash & me in the Turbo SxS class. Photo courtesy of Davey Kroll with DK28 Photography.

SxS RACE:

When it was time to start the SxS races, Cory lined up a half-dozen Expert SxS class racers on the front row, followed by seven Turbo SxS class racers, and eight competitors in the naturally aspirated SxS class. It was exciting to see such a strong turnout of side-by-sides!

After the SxS Expert class took off, I pulled Big Blue to the middle of the starting line. This class was made up mostly of Polaris RZR Turbos and Canam X3s plus one Wildcat (with an aftermarket turbo) driven by Richard Carter. Now there's a SxS you don't see everyday! Cash and I said a quick prayer for the safety of all racers, and then it was finally time to focus on Turn Number 1.

The flag went up, and off we went. Just like yesterday's Utility Amateur ATV race, John and I led the pack towards the first turn. John took the holeshot again with Cash and me nipping on his heals coming out of Turn Number 1. The dust hung heavy in the air as five angry turbo cars followed closely behind Cash and me. I felt good about our start and immediately let out a hearty, "YEEEHAW!" With Turn Number 1 in our rear mirror, we now had our work cut out for us as we faced 70 minutes of adrenaline-fueled racing.

Like yesterday, I followed John as closely as I could for as long as possible. But it wasn't long into the woods before he checked out. About halfway through Lap 1, we spotted John in the pecan trees area and I counted a 10-second gap. As the race progressed, we saw more and more side-by-sides parked along the edge of the course. No doubt, many were victims of the trees. Luckily, Big Blue kept going, and we held second position for the rest of the race. Mucho congrats to John for taking the win in the Turbo SxS class and to Brandon Byars for finishing third.

Sure, it would have been nice to take home at least one win during Round 1. But the way I see it, I dodged trees for 102 miles (including all three races, plus practice laps) on this fun track while surrounded by Cash and my TX4 racing family. I watched Cash get on the podium in his first ever ATV race, and I took home a one-of-a-kind "Triple Champ" plaque for winning three classes last year. Win or lose, it doesn't get any better than that!

LET'S GET CONNECTED

I hope you enjoyed this book! If so, **please do two small favors for me right now.**

First, please take two minutes to leave a short review of this book on Amazon and Goodreads. Online reviews help me find more readers. Your help in spreading the word about this book is greatly appreciated!

Second, please sign up for my reader's list at www.mikekowis.com/signup/ so that we can get connected. After you join, I'll occasionally share exclusive giveaways and announcements about my upcoming books and speaking engagements.

If you have any questions or wish to contact me about speaking to your group, I'm just an email away! Feel free to contact me anytime at mike.kowis.esq@gmail.com.

Cash and me smiling for the camera after one of our dusty SxS races. Photo courtesy of Mike Kowis.

Happy Trails!

ACKNOWLEDGEMENTS

This book would not have been possible without the extraordinary help and support of many folks, including my dear family, friends, and fellow off-road competitors. I would especially like to thank my two fun-loving children, Lauren and Cash, for having the courage to race with me from time to time. Of course, I can't forget to thank my lovely wife (and co-pilot in life) for encouraging me to go racing once a month. Honestly, I'm not sure if she really wants me to have fun or just wants to get me out of the house.

Many thanks to Curt Locklear for proofreading my manuscript. I would also like to give a shout-out to the talented photographers who generously gave me permission to print their photos in this book, including Davey Kroll with DK28 Photography (https://dk28photography.pixieset.com), Jodi Roush, and Thomi Beadnell. All of these talented individuals somehow turned my manuscript (also known as a *hot mess*) into something that Cash and I are very proud of.

Of course, I want to give a hearty *thank you* to Terry Deck and Cory Williams for granting me permission to re-print the TX4 race flyers in this book and for hosting fun and exciting off-road races in the Central Texas area. Without TX4, this book would not exist!

I want to offer my sincere appreciation to my long-time friend and movie aficionado, Robert "Ziggy" Parker, for his generous help in refining the "testimonials" for this book. In case you didn't figure it out, I made them up for my readers' amusement. If you didn't enjoy them, I blame Mr. Parker! If you loved them, I want to thank you in advance and let you know that Ziggy played a big part in making these zingers as humorous as possible.

Last, I want to give special thanks to Neslihan Yardimli at Book Cover Zone for the cover design and to Jason and Marina Anderson at Polgarus Studio for the interior print formatting and eBook conversion work.

It takes a skillful and dedicated team to create a book like this, and everyone who participated has my sincere appreciation for their contributions.

ABOUT THE AUTHOR

By day, **Mike Kowis, Esq.**, is a mild-mannered tax attorney at a Fortune 500 company in Texas. By night, he swaps a three-piece suit for a pair of tights and a shiny red cape and then begins his duties as a modern-day SUPERHERO (also known as "Adjunct Faculty Member") for one of the largest community colleges in the Lone Star State.

Specifically, Mike has practiced corporate tax law for a quarter-century, including the last 24 years at Entergy Services, LLC where he currently serves as Senior Tax Counsel. In addition, he has taught corporate tax and business law classes at Lone Star College-Montgomery for the past two decades. In his spare time, he writes books and competes in off-road races.

Mike holds a bachelor's degree and two law degrees, including a LL.M. in taxation from Georgetown University Law Center. He lives in Texas with his family, and his award-winning books are listed below.

In his debut book, *Engaging College Students: A Fun and Edgy Guide for Professors*, Mike shared the secrets to his success in the college classroom. Specifically, he provided 44 college teaching tips to help any teacher create a fun and lively learning environment, engage students in thought-provoking classroom discussions, motivate them to read the assigned materials, inspire them to attend all classes and stay till the final bell rings, and encourage them to use their critical thinking skills.

In his most popular book, *14 Steps to Self-Publishing a Book*, Mike explains how he turned the manuscript of his first book into a high-quality self-published book. He spells out 14 steps that anyone can follow to self-publish a top-quality book and sell it on websites like Amazon and BarnesandNoble.com. He also details the costs of his self-publishing journey and shares the top 10 lessons he learned from writing his first book.

In his first co-author project, Mike teamed up with seasoned author and book coach, Sharon C. Jenkins, to write a free eBook, *Maximize Your Book Sales With Data Analysis: The Cure for Authorship Analysis Paralysis*, which is intended to help self-published authors make the most of their book marketing efforts and tackle the dreaded authorship analysis paralysis.

In the following book, *Smart Marketing for Indie Authors: How I Sold my First 1,563 Books and Counting!*, Mike explains his proven book-selling formula and the 16 marketing tools he used to break 1,500 book sales within his first two years of being an independently-published author. Mike has used these same techniques to sell over 6,500 copies to date. He also provides the effectiveness rating for each marketing tactic along with the costs and time commitment involved.

During the pandemic, seasoned amateur competitor Mike Kowis launched *Texas Off-road Racing: A Father-Son Journey to a Side-by-Side Championship*, where he shares what off-road racing feels like from the driver's seat, plus how much money and time is required to compete in this harrowing motorsport. He also gives the gritty details of each side-by-side race that he and his teenage son competed in during their run for the 2019 Championship in a local off-road racing series. Whether you are a long-time off-road racer with 10 titles to your name, someone curious to learn about the sport, or a parent looking for exciting father-son activities, this book will surely entertain and enlighten you.

In his fifth book, *American Tax Trivia: The Ultimate Quiz on U.S. Taxation*, Mike challenges readers to 250 fun-filled trivia questions about federal income taxation. (Eureka! Did he just say "fun-filled" and "taxation" in the same sentence?) Specifically, this book quizzes readers on the rich and sometimes stormy history of U.S. tax law, the Internal Revenue Code, and important case law. Additional topics include amusing tax quotes, the United States Treasury Department, the Internal Revenue Service, tax forms, audits, politics, plus odds and ends that don't neatly fit into the above categories. Whether you are a seasoned tax practitioner, a neophyte taxpayer looking for an overview of U.S. taxation, a history buff, or just a trivia junky looking for your next fix, you will surely enjoy testing your knowledge of American taxation.

Texas Off-road Racing 2: The Battle for ATV and Side-by-Side Championships is the long-awaited sequel to *Texas Off-road Racing: A Father-Son Journey to a Side-by-Side Championship.* Here, Mike shares the gritty details of each round of ATV and side-by-side racing during his run for the 2022 championships in a brand new off-road racing series in Texas. Whether you are an experienced off-road racer, a newbie to the sport, or a parent looking for exciting activities to enjoy with your child, this book will surely entertain and enlighten you.

If you have any questions for Mike or would like him to speak at an event, please email him at mike.kowis.esq@gmail.com, find his author page on Facebook (Mike Kowis, Esq.), or visit his website at www.mikekowis.com.

www.ingramcontent.com/pod-product-compliance
Lightning Source LLC
Chambersburg PA
CBHW042314150426
43201CB00001B/2